Changing the Equation

Christ Changes Everything

Changing the Equation

Christ Changes Everything

Parochial homilies by
Father Michael Carvill, FSCB

HAB
Human Adventure Books

17105 Long Acres Lane
Odessa, FL 33556
http://humanadventurebooks.com/

First Edition 2021
Printed in the United States of America

Editor
Melissa Massy
Cover Design
Jacquie Colby

Library of Congress Cataloging-In-Publication Data
Names: Carvill, Michael, author
Title: Changing the Equation: Christ Changes Everything / Michael Carvill
Description: First edition | Odessa FL: Human Adventure Books, 2021
Keywords: Catholic Church, Sermons, Christianity, Religion
ISBN 978-1-94157-12-2 (trade paperback)

INTRODUCTION

Father Michael Carvill became a decisive person in the moment when I was beginning to lean towards a definitive choice of entering the Fraternity of St. Charles, the community of missionary priests of which we are both a part today. For this reason, in addition to being a brother for me, he is a dear friend, whom I esteem and admire.

It is with great joy that I present this collection of homilies, which are the expression of a profound human and Christian experience.

I often visit the houses of our priests who are serving in the United States, to share in a bit of their life and their work. I normally find them joyful and engaged, dedicated to the good of the people who have been entrusted to them. Looking at their faces, sometimes fatigued and at other times full of energy, I can see the greatness of a life given in order to respond to Christ, the beauty of a vocation that brings us to serve the Church in the midst of the generous American people.

Beyond regional differences, which are at times profound, the social context of the most influential nation in the world is generally difficult. Individualism and competition are largely proposed as positive values from childhood. Throughout the years, I have listened to many stories of men and women weakened by mutual extraneousness, often violated in that which is most sacred and intimate: their need to be loved. Even the proclamation of Christ is subtly opposed and there are many Christians who conform to the mentality of the world, embracing ideologies and demands that distance them from the Church. I have seen up close the wounds of a land in which confusion and lies have become widespread due to the attempt to impose an untrue idea of equality and of the fight against discrimination. Alone and battered by a continuous stream of propaganda that denies reality, that censures the most basic truths about human beings, and that lies about good and evil, many persons are increasingly fragile and insecure. Creating obstacles to the truest impulses of individuals, ideology brings to a society a diffused state of alienation that weighs souls down and tends to rob them of the taste for living.

These judgments can seem severe, and I certainly do not pretend that they are exhaustive. Still, a fact interrogates me, a clear perception that I had of many people with whom I have spoken: the fear to openly reveal one's own thoughts. It is fear of an invasive and potentially intolerant power.

In the heart of this land, the priests of the Fraternity of St. Charles are also present, together with who knows how many hidden points of life that God builds up without much fanfare, small signs that the world does not notice. And here is the surprise: a companionship, whether it be a parish or an ecclesial community, a group of families that form a fraternity, a house of priests or sisters, a group of young people who gather at school around a teacher who professes to be Christian, exerts a strong attraction on those whom they encounter. In these small companionships it is possible to be reborn; one can find a place of peace in a world that does not know repose and discover that a lived faith regenerates relationships and makes them more sincere. Being a witness of this miracle that happens repeatedly always leaves me in wonder. The experience of communion has the power to lead even the most exhausted or rebellious person back to good. Slowly, people begin again to hope and to love, to live in the truth, and even to rejoice.

The clearest image of all that I have described is that of a rushing river that flows from the communion of our houses; from the love lived in our Christian families, fed by the sacraments that we celebrate and receive. It is water that renews all that it touches, other houses, other families, other lives. It is a source that makes existence sacred, making stronger that which is healthy and restoring that which suffering has undermined.

"We are blessed, father," I have heard repeated time and time again by persons close to our priests. Through their eyes, I have seen the power and the sanctity of the work of God. He shows His humble force precisely in changed hearts, in the lives healed from solitude and desperation, in a rediscovered gratitude. Many thank us simply because we exist and live beside them. They thank us because we speak to them of

Christ and help them to know Him. It is He, in fact, who is the fount of that healing water that we can begin to experience.

On one of my trips to the States I was visiting Boston. During the Mass, while I listened to the homily of one of our priests, I was overtaken by a sudden thought: "The parishioners who frequent this Church have the opportunity to hear about Christ every day." Five minutes of commentary on the Gospel every day, to help them know a certain aspect of His person better, to indicate a path of meditation that can help them to remain in His company in the difficult hours of the new day. And so, I thought to myself: "This is what, in time, digs deep down into the hearts of these persons: constantly hearing these men speak of Christ. They are truly blessed because the lives of their priests have this center of a Person, alive, loved, desired, with whom they have an intimate and lively relationship." It is He who is the fundamental encounter of their existence; for this reason, they always speak of Him. They do not put sociological and psychological analyses first and foremost; they do not protest the faults of the Church, or the ways it lags behind or is rigid. They simply look at Christ with affection and wonder every time they take up the Gospel again to speak to their people.

Father Michael is one of these priests who is so strongly attached to the Lord of life. Further, he has the innate gift of easily finding some point of access to the page of the Gospel that the Church proposes for the daily celebration of the Eucharist. He does so with simplicity and immediacy, helping everyone immerse themselves in the narrated facts, in the diverse characters and situations. In this way, he brings us simultaneously before ourselves and before Jesus. While we listen to him, we feel seen in the depths of our heart; the state of our soul is laid bare, our preoccupations revealed, our objections come to the surface. And then we are placed before Christ in person; we can contemplate Him while as He speaks, responds, heals wounds and indicates the path.

It is not rare to hear Father Michael during the celebration of the Mass and experience a deep emotion, one that makes its way into the heart and fills it, gifting it with joy and encouragement. We are given an image or a thought that can sustain us in the coming hours, a suggestion on how to change something concrete in our lives, or a new perspective on the concrete reality of the Church. Every day parishioners can hear Father Michael's words at the Nativity of Our Lord church in Broomfield, CO. So often these homilies leave a mark in those who listen attentively. Through the years, the words spoken by Father Michael can deeply change the person who lends his ear to them.

Typically, Father Michael prepares for Mass without even writing a single line. He meditates the Scriptures in silence and then offers with spontaneity that which has struck him. Therefore, I am happy that some of his friends desired that words so precious would not be lost and have curated this collection to offer for the meditation of others.

In this initiative and the work that was necessary to complete it is expressed the gratitude of many towards a priest who testifies his love of Christ every day. We all need such witnesses because the change in society and the world begins from hearts that are converted to Christ.

Father Paolo Sottopietra
Rome, August 15, 2020
Solemnity of the Assumption of the Blessed Virgin Mary

ADVENT & CHRISTMAS

November 27, 2016
The First Day of Advent

READINGS

First Reading: Isaiah 2:1-5
Second Reading: Romans 13:11-14
Gospel Reading: Matthew 24:37-44

COLLECT

Grant your faithful, we pray, almighty God, the resolve to run forth to meet your Christ with righteous deeds at his coming, so that, gathered at his right hand, they may be worthy to possess the heavenly Kingdom. Through our Lord Jesus Christ, your Son, who lives and reigns with you in the unity of the Holy Spirit, one God, for ever and ever.

The Art of Giving Thanks

As I drove into the parking lot this morning, and as I saw all the cars, I said, "Well, at least many people know to whom to give thanks." And that led me then to the next thought, which was, "For what?" For what is it that we give thanks? I think sometimes we have a way of living our sense of thanksgiving that really contradicts the very art of what it is to give thanks. Sometimes our thanksgiving is a little bit naïve and a little bit inadequately pondered and comprehended. Sometimes we think of ourselves as these autonomous, self-sustaining beings to which from time to time God gives some nice big present. Maybe we go around the table, and we say, "What are you thankful for?" and we name a few of those gifts that God has given us during the year.

Now there is nothing wrong with that, but the gift of God goes far, far deeper. Our sense of gratitude has to penetrate and be aware of the gift of God in a far deeper way. When we think that maybe sometimes God gives us a gift, maybe sometimes he doesn't, maybe we have a misfortune, or maybe we have a fortune, we think we are in some kind of a fair-exchange relationship with God. Very often we find the sentiment that somebody is angry with God because something went wrong. This attitude really shows that in some sense we think we are God's equal, and he is just a big Santa Claus in the sky who from time to time gives us a present, and those things are the things we're grateful for. It is not so. We are certainly grateful for the blessings that happen to us in the days of our life, and there is absolutely nothing wrong with beginning our meditation on our gratefulness with some of the beautiful things that have happened to us throughout the year. There is nothing wrong with that. But if our gratitude stops there, then it is inadequate. If it stops there, it leaves us with a false idea of who we are and of our relationship with God.

The truth is that absolutely everything is gift. There is nothing about us that is not gift. There is nothing we have that we gave to or provided for ourselves. To help us to understand this, the Church contemplates two great gifts in the liturgy. These two great gifts could be called moments of gift in the life of a human being. The first great moment is the moment of our making, when God called us to being. The moment that God made me and invited me to this reality of existence. God made me beautifully and extraordinarily. The human being is made as a creature of such extraordinary beauty. When I am at the Grand Canyon or some beautiful place, one of the thoughts I always have is that any one human being is a greater, more magnificent, and more marvelous gift than these great scenes of a Grand Canyon or an angry ocean or whatever might communicate the power of God. In the things that we encounter in the world around us we find the pinnacle of God's creative genius, to use an anthropomorphic term. God's great creativity is most apparent in us, because we are made with a great destiny, which is life and communion with God. We are made for union with God. The gifts of our reason and freedom are an extraordinary thing. These extraordinary gifts, which are the attributes of our immortal soul, have their destiny in God. We need to be grateful for that. We need to ponder continually the extraordinary gift that is our vocation to be. Our vocation to be a human being. So that's the first gift that the Church recognizes in the liturgy.

Then the second gift, which the liturgy of the Church says is even greater than the first, is the Grace of our salvation in Jesus Christ. The gift of Christ comes to us and invites us to live with him. He invites us to fellowship with him. The second reading ended with the words that we have been called to life, to communion, with God, in Christ. And this, my friends, is truly an extraordinary gift. It is an extraordinary gift of communion with Christ in brotherhood. This gift is what we pray for at the Easter Vigil, in the Exsultet or Easter Proclamation, in Latin *Praeconium Paschale*. This is the hymn of praise sung before the Paschal candle during the Easter Vigil. One of the things that we say is, "Oh, happy fault." The reason that the Church uses this expression is precisely because this fault of original sin is what God uses as the pretext to bring us to an extraordinary new possibility of life. God offers us an extraordinary new possibility of life. The salvation that comes from Jesus is not just the restoration of what Adam and Eve lost by original sin, but it is the gift of an even greater, unimaginable step beyond the initial gifts that God gave to Adam and Eve. God gives us the gift of supernatural life by an indwelling of the very life of God himself. The Church recognizes that this gift of life in Christ is greater than the gift of our very being. This is the gift of belonging to Christ, of divine adoption. In our baptism we receive these gifts of the divine life. In baptism we became heirs to a destiny of communion with God.

My friends, as we live Thanksgiving Day, by all means we should contemplate the blessings that God gave us. As the funeral liturgy says, they are signs of our goodness. They are signs of our fellowship with the saints in Christ. Blessings are signs, but a sign remains incomplete unless it sends us to what it stands for. That's my invitation to you as we celebrate Thanksgiving Day today. I invite every one of us to let the signs indicate to us what they are signs of. When we remember around the table the things of which we are thankful this year, let them indicate to us what they are signs of, which is an extraordinary gift of our being and of our life in Christ.

As we celebrate our Thanksgiving Day today, let us ask that this sense of our gratitude to God be total. Let us ask that we really purge from our minds any sense of our own adequacy and that we realize that everything that we have is a gift. Let us remember that it is in virtue of these gifts that we can truly live. Let us ask the Lord for this overawing sense of gratitude, belonging, and adhering to the God who has given us everything.

November 29, 2015
First Sunday of Advent

READINGS

First Reading: Jeremiah 33:14-16
Second Reading: 1 Thessalonians 3:12—4:2
Gospel Reading: Luke 21:25-28, 34-36

COLLECT

Grant your faithful, we pray, almighty God, the resolve to run forth to meet your Christ with righteous deeds at his coming, so that, gathered at his right hand, they may be worthy to possess the heavenly Kingdom. Through our Lord Jesus Christ, your Son, who lives and reigns with you in the unity of the Holy Spirit, one God, for ever and ever.

Stay Awake in Your Heart

Perhaps the biggest danger that we face in our daily life is being distracted and not paying attention. When we don't take the time, in the silence, to pay attention to the deepest needs that we have, we end up trying to fulfill our yearning with small things that are incapable of fulfilling that yearning. That's what Jesus is warning us about today. He says:

> Do not let your hearts become drowsy, from perusing and drunkenness, and the anxieties of daily life, and that day catch you by surprise, like a trap.

When Jesus says this, he is warning precisely about this inattention to the religious dimension of our being, in the truest sense of that word. The religious dimension of our being realizes that the pieces of this world don't come together by themselves. The word *religion* has its etymological root in the word *religare,* which means *to bind fast*. Religion is that which binds things together again, that brings things whole again. That binding is a primary phenomenon in human beings. It is an instinct, a yearning, and a hunger that occurs in every single human being, whatever he or she might believe.

Whether a person is an atheist, or whether they may believe in any one of the religions that populate the face of the earth, this religious heart is there. Man can be defined as a religious animal. An animal that is looking for the rebinding of things when all things become one again.

Now Jesus came into the world precisely as the response to the religious need of man. The darkness that faces our human religiosity comes precisely from the fall of Adam and Eve and the consequent inability to see clearly. Jesus comes to shed light into this darkness. He sheds light in that darkness and answers the needs of our heart. Here is exactly where the problem comes. If our hearts are not awake, if we aren't paying attention to our hearts, then Jesus will always seem superfluous. When we think about the afterlife, perhaps we can hope Jesus will save us, but in our daily life he's superfluous. He doesn't really have any place because we aren't paying attention to our heart, and therefore we are quite content to live in the darkness. That is what Jesus is warning about on this very last Mass of this Church year. Already this evening when we celebrate the last Sunday Mass in ordinary time, here we will be wearing purple, and we will have begun the first Sunday of Advent. We conclude the year with this invitation to stay awake at the truest level of our being. We extend this invitation to not dismiss the pleading voice of our heart that wants something true, something great, something magnificent. Ultimately we want something fulfilling. When that heart is alive we will cling to Christ, and we will find it an ever relevant and continual accompanying criterion to our lives.

As we conclude this Church year, let us ask that we may enter the new year with hunger. The first part of Advent is most especially the season of this spiritual hunger. We already have it. The Church's year doesn't just end sharply. Bang! Even in ordinary time you begin to catch the themes of Advent. And indeed, we called out with this response, "Come, Lord Jesus." Let's ask that we might enter the Advent season awake to everything that our humanity needs. Let us ask that we be unwilling to content ourselves with the small things that are but a sign of God's goodness. Small things can be good because they are signs of his goodness, but they are useless if they are detached from that value that they have as signs of goodness.

Let us ask for these Graces as we conclude the year and prepare ourselves to begin the new year.

November 30, 2014
The First Sunday of Advent

READINGS

First Reading: Isaiah 63:16B-17, 19B; 64:2-7
Second Reading: 1 Corinthians 1:3-9
Gospel Reading: Mark 13:33-37

COLLECT

Grant your faithful, we pray, almighty God, the resolve to run forth to meet your Christ with righteous deeds at his coming, so that, gathered at his right hand, they may be worthy to possess the heavenly Kingdom. Through our Lord Jesus Christ, your Son, who lives and reigns with you in the unity of the Holy Spirit, one God, for ever and ever.

Jesus' Imperative: Be Alert!

In the Gospel, Jesus rarely uses the imperative. The imperative is that use of a verb where you give an order. You say, stop. Go. Do this. Don't do that. That's the imperative. And Jesus rarely uses an imperative, but here he does. And he uses it multiple times. Every time he is saying the same thing. He's saying to watch. Be attentive. Be aware. Look out. What is this attention that we need to pay? Well, we need to be really and truly alive as human beings. We need to let all the dynamics of our humanity live. We need not just be awake on the surface, responding to our most instinctive and immediate needs. We do need to delve down into the very depths of our soul and be aware of what it is that we truly need. What is it that we truly want? What is it that we truly hunger for? This is the special spirit of this Advent season. The spirit is looking forward to his coming. As somebody once said, no one can relate to the solution of a problem that they don't know exists, right? It is only when we know what a problem is that we can relate to its solution. If Jesus is coming at Christmas, then this Advent season, in its most immediate sense, is our preparation for that event. In our journey toward Christmas, toward the coming of Christ, how are we going to prepare for his coming?

The Advent season proposes that we prepare for Christmas by being alive in our hearts. We prepare by realizing that inside you and me, there is a deep and profound hunger for something that we don't find in this world. A hunger, we might say, for the infinite. A hunger for God. A yearning for

Love. All of these things manifest a depth in our soul that isn't simply resolved by the things of this world. And this is what Jesus means by *Be alert*! He warns us against living at the level of your most immediate instincts. Don't try to continually satisfy your human desire, your human need, or your human appetite simply with the created things you find around you. Ultimately, they will always disappoint. It's a very simple fact that nothing that occurs in nature or is made by human hand is able to answer the deepest yearning of your heart and my heart.

The Advent season is the time to let that heart speak. Let it say, "Not enough. Yes, I appreciate the good things of this world, but they are not enough for my soul." When we live in that way, alert, and awake, then when Jesus comes we will recognize him. We will welcome him because we know the problem, for which he has come as the solution: the problem of human happiness, the problem of human fulfillment. The problem of human completeness. The problem of true satisfaction in the depths of the soul. Jesus has come for that. If we don't really care about that, then we won't really care about Jesus. Then once again this Christmas we'll just go through the motions. So, the idea of this first week of Advent is to stir up and awaken in our souls the awareness of what it is that we want. And to awaken the awareness of our dissatisfaction.

The responsorial psalm for today was quite complicated, and if we didn't have that nice melody to follow, we probably wouldn't have been able to remember it each time we had to say it, because it has three different parts. It is worth watching those three different actions:

1) Lord, make us turn to you
2) Let us see your face
3) And we shall be saved (Psalm 80:8)

So, the first action is, "Make us turn to you." In the Gospel, as we have seen, there is this question about the hunger in the heart. Elsewhere in the Gospel Jesus uses a very simple term for it that we know very well from the Beatitudes. Jesus said, "Blessed are the poor in spirit" (Matthew 5:3). This deep, profound hunger that defines the heart of each one of us is that poverty of spirit. It is the poor in spirit that will turn when Jesus manifests himself. "Lord, make us turn to you." The first thing that Jesus wants us to do, and that we want Jesus to do, is make us turn to him. We want him. We desire him. We're not satisfied with the things of this world. Let us turn to you Lord. Attract us to yourself, O Lord. Draw us to yourself, O Lord, and then the second action will happen: we'll see your face. And when we see your face, the third action happened: we will be saved. That's the whole Christian journey right there. Jesus comes to win us to himself. He comes to attract us to himself.

December 8, 2014
Solemnity of the Immaculate Conception
of the Blessed Virgin Mary

READINGS

First Reading: Genesis 3:9-15, 20
Second Reading: Ephesians 1:3-6, 11-12
Gospel Reading: Luke 1:26-38

COLLECT

O God, who by the immaculate conception of the Blessed Virgin Mary, prepared a worthy dwelling or your son, grant, we pray, that, as you preserved her from every sin by virtue of the death of your son, which you foresaw, so, through her intercession, we, too, may be cleansed and admitted to your presence.

From the PREFACE

For you preserved the most Blessed Virgin Mary from all original sin, so that in her, endowed with the rich fullness of your grace, you might prepare a worthy Mother for you son, and signify the beginning of the Church, his beautiful Bride without spot or wrinkle.

She, the purest virgin, was to bring forth a son, the innocent lamb who would wipe away our offenses; you placed her above all others to be for your people an advocate of grace and a model of holiness.

Mary Full of Grace

> In the sixth month, the angel Gabriel was sent from God to a town of Galilee called Nazareth, to a virgin betrothed to a man named Joseph, of the house of David, and the virgin's name was Mary. And coming to her, he said, "Hail, Mary, full of grace! The Lord is with you." (Luke 1:26-28)

Mary pondered what sort of a greeting this might be. In other words, in very banal, modern parlance, you might say, "Huh? What? What could that possibly mean?" But Mary rightly identifies in this phrase of the angel's something truly extraordinary. This phrase of the angel is the reality that we celebrate today. From the beginning, from Adam and Eve to this moment, nobody had been worthy to bear the title that the angel gives to Mary. Not even Abraham, the father of faith. Not even Moses, or King David, or any of the other great holy people of the Old Testament could rightly have been addressed with the words *Hail, full of grace!*

Adam and Eve had shut the door on communion with God when they rebelled against him, and from that moment on, nobody was full of grace. Yes, the original imprint of God in man was still at least partly present, and therefore there definitely were moments of goodness. There were even great people. We just named three of them, Abraham, Moses, and David. David, of course, was famous also for his sins, but he is also famous for his relationship with God. Anyway, none of them, as I have said, could have been called full of grace, because grace was not in them. There was a relationship with God which he established, but they could not have been said to be full of grace. In fact, one of the great images of our faith from the Old Testament is of the crowds of the just, who wait at the gates of heaven for the coming of the salvific work of Christ. In our profession of faith, the one we say in the Rosary, in the Apostles Creed, we say, "And he descended into Hell." Perhaps some of you remember the old question in the Catechism about that Hell. It said this was not the hell of the damned to which one who has definitively abandoned and rejected God's grace is condemned. Rather, it was a place of expectation and waiting. A place of waiting for the grace that would open the gates of heaven and reconcile us with God. Mary received this grace before Moses, Abraham, or anyone else. She received this grace as she was conceived in the womb of her mother Anne. She received the life of grace. She received the gift of true friendship with God, and she lived all her life in fidelity to that friendship. We see in the story told in today's Gospel the emergence in her behavior of that friendship with God, that life of God in her soul which her soul affirmed.

Mary was not deprived of her freedom by the fact that she was full of grace. Mary, at any point, could have rejected God. In fact, Saint Bernard has written a beautiful meditation in which he freezes time at that moment after the angel has announced to Mary the plan of God. He imagines the time before Mary has yet had a chance to say her "Yes." He begins to plead and beg, expressing the voice of all of creation, crying out to Mary, begging that Mary will say her "Yes." Of course, Mary said her "Yes." Mary said her yes with the full assent of her humanity.

It's often been commented that this last phrase in today's Gospel, "And the angel departed from her" is another place that's very interesting to go in your meditation. Think about it in your contemplation of this scene in the Gospel. What was it like for Mary when the angel left? Suddenly, the four walls were there again. All of a sudden, everything was exactly as it had been before, only now Mary had this knowledge. Now Mary had this awareness of the great vocation to which she had been called. And she was aware of the great event of the salvation of the world that had begun in her very body. Then she had to go and face the world. There was no mark on her. She had no certificate, no excuse, and no permission for any of the things she had to face. She had to go and face them as a human being among her fellow human beings. First her husband-to-be, and then, slowly but surely, the rest of the world would come to know Mary in the greatness of this vocation which had been given to her. We would truly, as she herself says in her Magnificat, call her blessed. All generations will call her blessed, in answer to the scriptures. Sometimes our Protestant brothers and sisters might ask us, "Where on earth did you come up with the Immaculate Conception? Where is that in the Bible?" Well, we just read it, didn't we? We read it right here in the angel's words, "Hail full of grace." Right there, the angel proclaims this doctrine. In the temporal line of history, even though Christ has not yet died on the cross or risen from the dead to vanquish evil forever, Mary is full of grace.

And Mary receives this grace as the Collect of today's Mass tells us. Mary receives this grace in an anticipation of the graces that the very son, soon to be born of her, will win through the Paschal mysteries of his passion, death, and resurrection. Mary received this grace and is the model for us. In the Preface of this Mass, which is particular to this feast, we find recapitulated in beautiful language all the great mysteries that begin in the event of Mary's visitation.

Another thought that is worth mentioning is that Mary's Immaculate Conception is a dogma of the Church; it's *de fide*. It's an integral part of the faith. If we are Catholic, we believe it. It's part of our Catholic faith. And within that, included in that, is an implication about the humanity of the unborn. In this event is that belief that we have always had as Catholics, and of which we have always been great witnesses in the world these last 50-60 years now, to the humanity of the unborn. We are witnesses to the human dignity of the unborn from the moment of conception until natural death, as we say in our prayers. Only that which is human, only that which is a person, can sin. A thing cannot be guilty of sin. Many things might not work, and we might say they are useless, but we don't call them sinners. We don't call our dogs sinners even when they might do the worst things dogs can do. When dogs dirty the house or bite somebody, even for that we don't call them evil. We do punish them to train them, but we don't attempt to tell them they have sinned. Because only the person can sin. Only the person endowed with freedom can sin. So, if Mary was conceived without original sin, it implies that possibility of sin was there from the beginning. A little group of cells isn't capable of sin. Only a human being.

On this feast day we can remember and be more confirmed in our belief and witness of the dignity of human life from the first moment of conception. And that's another intention for which we can pray.

December 9, 2014

READINGS

First Reading: Isaiah 40:1-11
Gospel Reading: Matthew 18:12-14

COLLECT

O God, who by means of Saint Juan Diego showed the love of the most holy Virgin Mary for your people, grant, through his intercession, that, by following the counsels our Mother gave at Guadalupe, we may be ever constant in fulfilling your will. Through our Lord Jesus Christ, your Son, who lives and reigns with you in the unity of the Holy Spirit, one God, for ever and ever.

Saint Juan Diego's Simplicity of Heart

> It is not the will of my heavenly father that even one of these little ones shall be lost. (Matthew 18:14)

The passion of God for us, for our human condition, and for the salvation of each one of us, is one of the most extraordinary things we have come to know through revelation. We know that God deeply desires, yearns for, and wants that each and every one of us might have the fullness of life. We are not celebrating a liturgical feast today, but the calendar reminds us that it is only a few days before the feast of Our Lady of Guadalupe. It recalls to us Saint Juan Diego, the young man to whom the blessed Virgin appeared in that wonderful miracle. This is what we celebrate on Friday, the Feast of Our Lady of Guadalupe. Juan Diego and his story illustrates exactly this desire and passion of God: that every one of us should be saved.

The people of Mexico at that time were in the grip of a terrible religious fear. They feared that if they failed to sacrifice the right number of young human beings to God, then God would be angry and destroy them. Nothing could free them from this religious fear, it was like a national scruple. It was something that bound the conscience of those poor people in such a way that they could not free themselves from it. The Franciscans' mission to preach the Gospel began with their arrival, along with the conquistadors to the New

World. However, because of this terrible fear the Franciscans were unable to make much headway. They won a few converts, but not many.

Among the few converts they won was this young man Juan Diego, who began to believe in Jesus and his salvation. However, Juan was still not completely free. In his story we find that when his uncle was sick, and our Blessed Mother was waiting to appear to him on the top of a hill, Juan decided to take a different route as he went into Mexico City to find help for his uncle. So the Blessed Mother came down the opposite side of the hill of Tepeyac to encounter "Juanito" as he was hurrying to Mexico City. Our Blessed Mother was intent on reassuring him that this event of her visitation was a revelation of God's love to the people of Mexico. It was an encounter to open the people of Mexico to the Gospel. Juan Diego went to the top of the hill where he received roses from Our Lady. He also received, unbeknownst to him, the miraculous impression of the Blessed Mother on his cloak. This impression was only revealed when Juan finally opened his cloak to show the Bishop the roses, that he had picked in the middle of winter. Through that great miracle the Gospel was opened to the Mexican people. In a very, very short time the Mexican people became one of the great branches of the Church.

I comment on this precisely because to me it shows again this desire of the heavenly Father that not a single human being should fail to reach that fullness of life for which each one of us was made. That continual initiative of God pleads with human freedom to let go of all the false values and fears and to adhere, with simplicity, to the attractiveness of Christ and of the salvation that he brings. In a previous homily I drew the image of those hills and valleys of which John the Baptist speaks, quoting the prophet Isaiah. The filling in of the valleys and the leveling of the hills could be seen precisely as this freedom from false values (the hills) and false fears (the valleys). These hills and valleys get in the way and don't allow us to see with simplicity of heart that our Lord is waiting, begging, and longing for us simply to come to him and to receive the gift of life. So, as we continue our Advent journey, let us ask that through the intercession of Saint Juan Diego, we might have the grace of this simplicity of heart that sees things as they truly are and therefore sees the Lord. Give us a heart that sees our Lord and Savior Jesus Christ clearly and plainly. Give us the grace to see that which is truly to be preferred, that in which we can find our greatest good.

December 10, 2014
Wednesday of the Second Week of Advent

READINGS

First Reading: Isaiah 40:25-31
Gospel Reading: Matthew 11:28-30

COLLECT

Almighty God, who commands us to prepare the way for Christ the Lord, grant in your kindness, we pray, that no infirmity may weary us as we long for the comforting presence of our heavenly physician. Who lives and reigns with you in the unity of the Holy Spirit, one God, for ever and ever.

The Peace Gained from Conversion

The way of Satan, the way of autonomy from God, the way of the self-made man, is hard and arduous. It ultimately produces nothing that satisfies the human soul. Jesus comes and finds a world entirely struggling under this burden of being alone after a broken relationship with God. He invites us, each one of us, to a new way of living a much easier life. Jesus' way of life is much more beautiful and continually produces fruit that is surprising, agreeable, and delightful to our hearts. This new way of life is that for which our hearts are made. It is this invitation of Jesus that is at the very core of the Gospel. The invitation is to re-evaluate, to decide again, to make a different decision about the way to face life. This changing of mind, this changing of heart, is called a *conversion.* We very often think the word *conversion* means becoming Protestants, or Catholics, or something like that. However, conversion is a continual ongoing process in which we change our mentality. Conversion means that we change our thinking about things. We change our conception of things. We change the strategy with which we face the trials of life. This conversion places Christ as the center of our lives and relies on him for the fulfillment of our hearts. In this way we can truly go through the world carrying a burden that is light. This new way of living doesn't mean we shirk our responsibilities or that we don't engage with the reality of life, but it means that we engage it in a new way, with a new heart and a new certainty. If you think that in one little situation you know everything, it often leads to the worst arguments you can get into. We manage to convince ourselves that, at that moment, everything we need to know is in front us and that we know what tomorrow brings. Then we fight for our position. We argue with our spouses or whoever, because we think it's all going to play out the way we think. In that moment everything else disappears. All we see is that one little conflict, and we feel this totally compelling need to win. To come out on top. This is just a parable, though, of the way we live our lives. Because the thing that makes us not free, the thing that burdens us, is that we think we are alone. And we think that our happiness plays out in the successes, the failures, and the victories that we have in this world. But instead, the fulfillment of our lives has already been given. It is already here. He has already given himself to us. And therefore, we can truly be at peace. And that peace puts us in the human position that is most adequate to facing the circumstances of life.

So, this passage in the Gospel, "Come to me you who labor and are overworked, and I will give you rest" (Matthew 11:28) doesn't mean a disengagement from the commitments of our life. This passage doesn't mean that we won't continue to struggle and work to be great in whatever field of endeavor we are in, it just means that we know that victory has already been given. Therefore, we go to those tasks with peace. We go to those tasks with certainty.

This reminds me of a little scene I once saw. It was a group of kids who were over at the church in Massachusetts to volunteer. There was a huge pile of autumn leaves outside the front of the church, and I gave them rakes and brushes and sacks. I said, "Put the leaves in the sacks." Immediately I realized that not only did they have no clue how to do it, they weren't sure if they could do it. So, they were literally doing nothing. They just kind of moved their rakes around, but there was no concept or the possibility of completion. As I watched them, I said to myself, "You know, that's the way we face life. We face the trouble of life already convinced of our defeat." Whereas the truth is that we need to face life convinced of victory, because victory has been given. In that which counts in life, victory has already been won for us. That is what Jesus is inviting us to do. He is inviting us to live as people of his victory and in his victory. He invites us to live confidently in his victory. I decided at that moment, with the kids and the leaves, that instead of urging them or encouraging them, or saying, "Come on, try and get it done now," I would take five minutes and show them how you rake leaves and put them in a bag. And then I just went away and immediately they wanted more leaves. They said, "Father, are there any more leaves we can sweep?" Because once they knew it could be done, and that they could do it, they went to work with all their energy and all the vitality of their young lives. We need that too. We need to know that in Christ, everything is accomplished. Then we can go to the tasks of our lives, and we can engage them in a new way, with a new confidence, with a new trust, and a new energy. We could truly be free.

The word that Christ uses for this experience of trusting him is *freedom*. As we celebrate our Holy Mass today, let us ask that we may come to the Lord, we who labor and are heavily burdened. Let us ask that we may come to the Lord and that we might enjoy his yoke which is easy, and his burden, which is light.

December 16, 2014
Tuesday of the Third Week of Advent

READINGS

First Reading: Zephaniah 3:1-2
Gospel Reading: Matthew 21:28-32

COLLECT

O God, who through your Only Begotten Son have made us a new creation, look kindly, we pray, on the handiwork of your mercy, and at your Son's coming cleanse us from every stain of the old way of life. Through our Lord Jesus Christ, your Son, who lives and reigns with you in the unity of the Holy Spirit, one God, for ever and ever.

PRAYER AFTER COMMUNION

Replenished by the food of spiritual nourishment,
we humbly beseech you, O Lord,
that, through our partaking in this mystery,
you may teach us to judge wisely the things of earth
and hold firm to the things of heaven.
Through Christ Our Lord.

True Poverty of Spirit

> There was a man who had two sons. He went to the first and said, "Son, go and work today in the vineyard." "I will not," he answered, but later he changed his mind and went. (Matthew 21:28)

Another rendering of the phrase "he changed his mind" is: He thought better of it. Thank God that we can think better of it. Perhaps you know from your theology that the angels don't have this ability because they have pure and perfect knowledge. Therefore, once an angel decides, it's decided. They can't change their minds. Their freedom is perfect, but their freedom is singular. Today we might even call it a binary option, right? Whereas we are human beings who live a relationship with reality that leads us, and draws us, and slowly wins us over.

Jesus used this very method himself by coming into the world. He did this so that there would be something in the world that would truly make us *think better of it* and we would be persuaded. He came into the world so that our resistance would be overcome by the nature of Jesus himself. He himself said when he was raised upon the cross that he would finally have the convincing power to draw us all to himself. A part of that *being drawn to Christ* is the poverty of spirit, which is particularly emphasized in this period that we might call *outer Advent* that ends today. This is the last day of the first part of Advent. As of tomorrow, we begin the novena of Christmas. The liturgy makes a radical shift and we already begin to participate in the joy of Christ's coming. In this part of Advent, up to December 16, we are encouraged to discover in our hearts the true insufficiency of ourselves to the fulfillment of the great desire of our hearts. It is in that poverty of spirit that we can again and again make a discovery, becoming ever more persuaded that to do the Lord's will is in our interest. We become ever more certain that to do the Lord's will is what truly corresponds to us.

In today's Gospel, the first son said immediately that he would go. But somewhere in his heart he really didn't believe that going there to the field, working and doing his father's will, was what would make him happy. So, he didn't go. The second son said, "I will not go." So, his most immediate action was resistance. However, consideration, pondering, contemplation, relationship with God, and prayer changed his mind. All of these things are part of our spiritual journey in this life that leads to *thinking better of it*. Yet if we continually fill our lives with distraction and diversion, we will never think better of it. To think better of it is to spend time, to pay attention, to watch, to be attentive, and to see what is really happening. In the prayer that I read by mistake at the beginning of the Mass, which is the concluding prayer of the Mass, it asks that we may be able to judge wisely the things of this world. This means the same thing as *thinking better of it*. Throughout this whole outer-Advent period, ending today, we have that same prayer that asks that we may judge wisely the things of this world, and so cling to the things that endure forever.

What does it mean to judge wisely the things of this world? Well, ultimately it means to think better of it. Better in this case means to think more and more profoundly, more deeply, and more truly of it. Not to just judge things on the surface, but to judge the things of this world wisely. To discover what the things of this world can contribute to us. It also means to understand what the things of this world can't contribute to us. We will discover, if we pay real and true attention, that they do play a part. If we think well of the things of this world, we will discover their true glory, their true goodness, and their true usefulness. They serve us in our relationship with that which endures forever. Let us ask the Lord that we may become aware of the truth of all the things in our life—that they are given to us as instruments, to assist us on the journey toward our destiny.

December 20, 2015
Fourth Sunday of Advent

READINGS

First Reading: Micah 5:1-4A
Second Reading: Hebrews 10:5-10
Gospel Reading: Luke 1:39-45

COLLECT

O God, eternal majesty, whose ineffable Word the immaculate Virgin received through the message of an Angel and so became the dwelling-place of divinity, filled with the light of the Holy Spirit, grant, we pray, that by her example we may in humility hold fast to your will. Through our Lord Jesus Christ, your Son, who lives and reigns with you in the unity of the Holy Spirit, one God, for ever and ever.

God's Plan is the Solution

Is God's way better? Or is man's way better? Are we able to assure our happiness, our satisfaction, the fullness of our life, our daily joy, our contentment more by taking care of it ourselves? Or are we going to accomplish that end more readily by obeying God's law? Are we able to assure our happiness by following God, by adhering to God, and by being with God? This is the great, great question which has always stood over humanity.

Right from the beginning, Adam and Eve, as they lived in the garden of Eden, among all the material bliss that the Lord had given them, really became doubtful about the answer to this question. Under the influence of the tempter, of Satan, they had begun to think that they could do a better job of securing their own happiness, securing their own fulfillment, securing their own contentment. Adam and Eve thought they could secure for themselves a good day. Because we shouldn't think of happiness as something abstract. We need to think of happiness as the real happiness we experience when we have a good day, a day that we really enjoy.

Adam and Eve had begun to think that, well, perhaps that fruit is necessary. Perhaps I must have that fruit, because that is what Satan's temptation to Adam and Eve was. God is keeping happiness from you by not letting you eat that fruit. You eat that fruit and you'll get your happiness. As long as you don't eat that fruit, God is keeping happiness away from you. He's depriving you of something. And Adam and Eve bought it. They bought the temptation and chose to eat the forbidden fruit. We too are always faced with that question, again and again and again. Every moment of our lives we face the same question: is our happiness more readily secured by our own wits, capacities, powers, and strengths? Or is our happiness more readily secured by our adherence to our God? That's the great question that stands over all of human history.

Now, until the coming of Jesus, nobody chose perfect adherence to God. Elsewhere I have dealt with the biblical story of evolution and creation, and I'm not going to go there – that's resolvable. The stories are here to help us understand the meanings of things. So, beginning with Adam and Eve and onward, no human being had been able to entirely and truly bet on God's will as the possibility of life and happiness. And therefore, no human being in the history of the world had ever fully, totally, and completely participated in the human condition to its full. Every single human being, beginning with Adam and Eve and until the coming of Christ, had their humanity eclipsed. Every single human being had their humanity betrayed. They betrayed the ultimate fulfillment of their happiness. There were indeed great heroes, and there were indeed great people who tended toward the good in many, many moments in their lives. We think of Abraham, father of faith. We think of King David. We think of so many people in the Old Testament, all who strived, in some way, to accept God. However, not one of them could ever entirely and completely bet on God's plan as *the* solution to life. *The* plan of life. Jesus came for this. And that's what Saint Paul is telling us. That's what his reflection is about in the letter to the Hebrews that we read today. He's showing us that Jesus of Nazareth, the Son of God, entered the world and lived entirely, totally, and perfectly, the will of his Father. He was obedient to the Father up to the point of death. There was no separation between Jesus of Nazareth and the will of his Father in heaven.

Through this human being, who lived in his humanity, which he shared with us in all things but sin, in his humanity he lived for us a re-creation. He lived a life that was true. He lived a life that was fulfilled. And that includes the cross. It doesn't eliminate the cross; it includes the cross. The question we have to ask ourselves is whether Jesus' plan of life was better than those many plans that we come up with to secure our happiness without this obedience to God.

Jesus came and was obedient to the Father. This is what we celebrate this Christmas. We celebrate the beginning of a whole new epoch in the history of the world. A whole new dimension coming into the history of the world. One of us, our brother, our savior Jesus Christ, came among us, and lived life to the full. Lived every experience in life, going to the very core and depths of that experience, which was his belonging to his Father. He invites us to share that life. That is why the infant John the Baptist leaps! John leaps in the womb of his mother, when Our Lady, with Jesus in her womb, comes into Elizabeth's presence as we read in the Gospel today. And this leaping for joy is a sign. It's a sign that in some way stands between the Old and New Testament. The

Old Testament stands as a struggle to figure out and to finally put life back into place the way it should be. And the New Testament brings the Savior, who comes into the world to effect that restoration in its totality.

John the Baptist leaps for joy because salvation has come to the world. And my friends, that salvation is the accomplishment of the will of the Father. It is the final setting aside of all those short cuts that we think we can make. All that grasping that we think will lay hold of our happiness and the fullness of life independent of our relationship with God. It doesn't happen. It always escapes our grasp. No matter how many times we reach out to grab happiness independent of God, we always end up finding that our hands are really empty when we've finished grasping. When we are in the throes of the grasp, we think, "This is it!" But when the grasp is over, the next day we look and we say, "My hands are empty. I have nothing. I ended up with empty hands." John the Baptist leapt for joy in the womb of his mother because he understood that now and forever that drama was over. Now and forever that drama would be resolved. Jesus, the Son of God, had taken a body. God had taken our condition to himself, in all things but sin. Jesus would live in perfect conformity with the will of his Father. And now a new model, a new possibility for humanity would be open to us.

Throughout the year we will have plenty of opportunity to reflect on that journey that Jesus invites us to make with him. However, today is the last Sunday of Advent, and this very week we will celebrate the birth of Jesus in Bethlehem. This last week, the Church invites us to delve more deeply into that question: Are we better on our own? Or with God? Look, we're all here in the Church, and we could just say, "We're all here in the Church, Father. We've made our choice, right?" And to a certain extent that is true. However, the human question always goes deeper. It is true, our presence here is a profound, deep, and strong sign of what it is that we prefer. But what is it that we really prefer, and what is it that we really want? We have to allow the question to penetrate to the very depths of our soul. We have to become profoundly convinced because it is still possible that there will be a rift between our presence here around the altar on Sunday morning and what we do when we go out there in the world for the other six days of the week. Are we profoundly convinced that this is the best place? Are we profoundly convinced that what happens here, that the Eucharist which we will momentarily receive from the altar is truly the food of life? Are we convinced that it is in relationship with that life that we find our very, very best chance for a full, good, holy, happy, complete, and joyful life?

My friends, this is the season to banish from our hearts all those doubts that we have that we might do better on our own. Because every sin, if you think about it, is ultimately that. What is a sin except our decision to do it our way, rather than his way? That's what sin is.

So, let us ask then, as we celebrate the holy Mass, for this grace as we continue the journey through the Advent season. Let us ask for this grace to come to our senses and to understand that God's way is the only possibility because we are his creatures. He made us. We belong to him. Let us ask that we may come to know, in all certainty, the profound truth of our gesture, the one that each one of us made in coming here this morning to Mass. Let us ask that we may be profoundly convinced of this and let us ask that we may banish from our hearts every doubt.

December 25, 2015
Christmas Day

READINGS

First Reading: Isaiah 9:1-6
Second Reading: Titus 2:11-14
Gospel Reading: Luke 2:1-14

COLLECT

O God, who gladden us year by year as we wait in hope for our redemption grant that, just as we joyfully welcome your Only Begotten Son as our Redeemer, we may also merit to face him confidently when he comes again as our Judge. Who lives and reigns with you in the unity of the Holy Spirit, one God, for ever and ever.

The Birth of Beauty Itself

How is it, my friends, that after 2,000 years and more, now, this great holiday, this great feast, is never reduced. This feast continues to grow, and it continues to draw us to this scene. It continues to draw us to this place and to this contemplation. To face this reality that we celebrate tonight, the birth of our Savior in a stable in Bethlehem. The world has changed so radically, and so many times. Even in our times we see the world changing. Yet once again tonight we gather here in thousands, literally, just in our church. At our 4 PM Mass this evening, there were people everywhere, all the way down the stairs, everywhere. Every inch was taken. There were people sitting everywhere. At our 6 PM, our 8 PM, this Mass, tomorrow morning, the same. What is it that draws us so intensely and so joyfully to this moment? Why is it that we feel we must be here tonight? Why is it that we feel we must come to contemplate this scene?

I think we can answer this question with one word, which I would like to reflect upon for a moment, and that is the word *beauty*. We human beings are attracted by beauty. In fact, that's the very thing that beauty is – it's that which attracts. As the body has its senses, the soul has its senses. And we learn the senses of the soul: our intellect, the capacity for truth; and will, the capacity for good. These two capacities of intellect and will are intertwined in our humanity and are united totally and perfectly. These capacities represent the movement toward beauty that is so decisive in the human person. All we need to do is look at the travel logs and the travel magazines to see that anywhere on the face of this planet of ours where we find a little bit of beauty, there pop up the hotels and the resorts and all these things because we always seek to go to beauty.

In every aspect of our lives, we are drawn by beauty. This beauty, like so many other things, has an analogous form. While some things are beautiful in a very simple and unpretentious way, there is one thing that is beauty itself, and that is our God. And he is the one who is born in the stable in Bethlehem. He is the one whose birth we celebrate this evening. The birth of beauty itself. And I think it's precisely in this beauty that we find ourselves continually drawn. We find that we need to come, and come, and come again to this scene to contemplate this beauty. It is our place. It is a place that somehow, to the soul of each one of us, offers promise and hope. And if, perhaps, we haven't worked out all of the implications of this hope, of this beauty, of this attraction, of this something in our hearts that made us decide to be here tonight, nonetheless, we are vulnerable, and therefore we have been moved. That vulnerability to beauty is our greatest gift. That vulnerability to beauty is the greatest trait of our humanity. And he comes, beauty himself, the one who is all beautiful, the one who corresponds entirely to that heart of ours.

He that desires the good and desires to know the truth finds in this world nothing that is lasting beauty. We catch glimpses of beauty throughout this world. These days before Christmas, so many things beckon to our appetite and seem to say to us,

"This will satisfy you." However, we know in our heart of hearts that nothing on sale at the mall, nothing you can order on Amazon or anywhere else, nothing we can acquire or accomplish ourselves is beauty itself. Therefore, our eyes are always raised a little, somehow, in the depths of our soul. We still expect, we still wait, we still long. We're still looking out for a great chance for ourselves. We do this regardless of how successful we may have been. Maybe we have become very wealthy. Maybe we have become very powerful, but yet we continue to raise our eyes and scan the horizon, expecting. Expecting something more, no matter how much we have. Our hearts want something more.

Well, my friends, this night we celebrate the gift of that something more. Of that thing for which our hearts are made. That thing that alone, entirely, completely, and totally corresponds to the deepest yearning and desire that is the very nature of our self, our heart. It's for this reason that we come, again and again. It is for this reason that none of the forces of history that have sought to wipe away this reality of ours have wiped it away. Kingdoms and empires. Empires upon which the sun had never set, wiped away and gone, like the flash of an eye. Yet this event remains. Once again tonight we gather here around this beautiful and extraordinary scene. Once again harkening to the voice of those angels over Bethlehem, whose words we have sung this very night. We come. We make haste. To gather here. To watch.

My friends, this beauty, of its very nature, invites us to come and to draw close. It is not enough that we catch a glimpse of it from time to time. This time of year, so many come to church who perhaps throughout the year don't come. Tonight's birth is an invitation to all to truly draw close. Because, my friends, this beauty shines forth in its radiance in a way that draws us all here. It draws us, so we can enter into that beauty, and so that the journey of beauty can take place in our lives. This beauty shines so that our lives may be made entirely new. Entirely reborn. That we may become entirely glad. Entirely full of joy. That we may have peace. Yes, my friends, we do come here tonight because there is a promise. Perhaps, even those of us who are here most frequently have not yet even really begun to penetrate the great depths of that beauty that this Savior, Our Lord Jesus Christ, has for those of us who will truly come to him. He invites us. Tonight, his birth is an invitation. It is an initiative of God to extend a relationship to us so that we can live in an entirely new way. Christianity is not meant to be one of the religions of the world. Christianity is not meant to be a lifestyle or a way of doing things, it is meant to be an entirely new creation. The fact that we can so easily and so often perceive it as just one more approach, just one more lifestyle, just one more religion, shows that, even though we are vulnerable to the beauty, and though we have gathered here tonight around the altar, we have not yet begun to penetrate entirely and deeply into that mystery which is his life. The life to which he calls us and invites us.

This coming year I am going to talk more about this invitation in my homilies. I want to talk more about what that journey is like and what the response to Jesus is. Let us talk more about what it means to give your life to Christ and what it means to be with Christ. What does it mean to pay attention to this beauty? What does it mean to be held by this beauty? Let us be held riveted in our very hearts by this beauty. Let us come to discover in him the endless treasures of beauty. When I say we have not really begun to penetrate the mystery entirely, this is applicable even to the most holy among us. If Mother Teresa was sitting here, she would want to hear more right away. She would immediately accept that we haven't even begun yet to satiate ourselves entirely with the beauty that has drawn us here this evening.

Let us ask then, as we celebrate this birth, that this beauty may take hold of us. That we may not just peek in the door, from time to time, and say, "Oh, how lovely." Let us ask that we might be drawn entirely, completely into the house of the Lord. Let's ask for this grace tonight for ourselves and for one another as we celebrate the glorious night of the birth of our savior.

January 1, 2015
The Octave Day of Christmas
Solemnity of the Blessed Virgin Mary, the Mother of God

READINGS

First Reading: Numbers 6:22-27
Second Reading: Galatians 4:4-7
Gospel Reading: Luke 2:16-21

COLLECT

O God, who through the fruitful virginity of Blessed Mary bestowed on the human race the grace of eternal salvation, grant, we pray, that we may experience the intercession of her, through whom we were found worthy to receive the author of life, our Lord Jesus Christ, your Son. Who lives and reigns with you in the unity of the Holy Spirit, one God, for ever and ever.

Get Real!

Some of you might remember Father Michele who said Mass these last couple of weeks. Well, this morning I dropped him off at the airport and as I was coming back, I was saying my rosary. I was about to begin when I said, "hmm, Thursday, the Luminous Mysteries." But then I remembered a document of the Church regarding the rosary, contained in a book you can buy called *The Directory on Works of Piety and Devotion.*[1] In this official document it says that when there are big feasts, then instead of saying the rosary for that day according to the normal schedule, you should instead say the rosary that the feast expresses. So, I said to myself, "Does this great feast express one of the mysteries of the rosary?" And then, of course, I immediately thought of the Joyful Mysteries.

In the Joyful Mysteries we have the annunciation of Jesus' birth to Mary. Then we have the visitation of Mary to Elizabeth, and indeed it's Elizabeth who first addresses Mary with the title with which we're celebrating her today. Elizabeth said, "Why am I so favored, that the mother of my Lord should come to me?" (Luke 1:43) And this is the first place in scripture as well as the first place in the history of the

---

[1] Directory on Popular Piety and the Liturgy, Vatican City, December 2001, http://www.vatican.va/roman_curia/ congregations/ccdds/ documents/rc_con_ccdds_doc_20020513_vers-direttorio_en.html

Church where we find that title with which we celebrate Mary today, used when Elizabeth addresses her as the Mother of God.

And then, of course, we have the birth of Jesus and the other two events that take place a little later. We have the presentation in the temple and the finding in the temple. So, certainly the rosary I was going to say was the Joyful Mysteries. As I thought of that I also recognized that in some way all of the mysteries are appropriate to today. The whole rosary. Maybe I should say twenty decades today, I don't know. We'll see how the day plays out. Because one of the things about today's feast is that it unites, entirely and totally, Christ and his mother. The title of today's feast is his mother's feast, yet the feast is also his. In some sense, I suppose, all feasts belong to Jesus in the liturgical year. However, this feast is his in a very special way because this title, *Mary the Mother of God* has a long history in the Church, and it expresses who Jesus is.

There was a lot of controversy in the first centuries about who Jesus is. In the first decades of the life of the Church, Jesus' identity was testified to by the apostles themselves who communicated their certainty to those communities they founded and the communities that derived from these communities. In these communities there was no doubt about who Jesus was. The claim about the identity of Jesus, that Jesus was actually the Son of God, was so great that it overwhelmed those who approached Christianity in a tentative way. The claim that he was really, and truly, God in the flesh had to be mitigated. Many times, they tried to say, "Oh, come on. We'll believe you, and we'll stay with you Christians if you accept that Jesus was a special messenger of God. That God took possession of the body of a human being and spoke through him." Although there were many different ways they tried to mitigate the great claim that's at the very center of our Christian faith, it all centered around the idea that Jesus was something less than God himself.

One of the most ancient prayers we know in the Church is a prayer called Sub Tuum Praesidium (Beneath Thy Protection). It's a prayer that, in fact, we priests say when we get in the car to go on any trip. We always say this prayer for blessing because it's a prayer of the wayfarer. From the very first centuries, this prayer is the first place in which the historians can find Mary addressed again, as Elizabeth did, *Sancta Dei Genitrix* – the Holy Mother of God.

This title always had with it this feeling that maybe it's excessive. This was not so for the Christians or those who belonged and lived in obedience of faith within the Christian community. However, in the first, second, third, and fourth centuries, the Church is in rapid expansion. The people who come to the Church continually want to whittle away this core claim of faith that Jesus is God. It was finally resolved in the year 431. The Great Council of Ephesus addressed Mary and declared that this title, Mother of God, was the right title for Mary. The Council decreed that it not only defines correctly what the relationship between Mary and God is, but it also defines correctly to whom she gave birth. Mary's title expresses unequivocally that the one to whom she gave birth was not a vessel of God, was not a sign of God, was not a messenger of God, but was God himself. Holy Mary, Mother of God. That's what we say, and that's what we mean. That is the core of our belief, that God himself has come among us. Throughout this coming year we will have many opportunities to meditate upon the consequences of this event, which contains within it everything that gives hope to the world. Without it, the world would ultimately not have hope.

I wanted to suggest one final thought today about this mystery and its consequences. It comes from my earlier reflection on the way back from the airport when I was saying the rosary. It says here in the Gospel that we just read, that, "Mary pondered all of these things in her heart." We find this phrase about Mary repeated several times in the Gospel. Mary pondered in her heart all of these things that were happening. That's where the rosary is born. The rosary is a sharing in Mary's pondering. It is a way to go with Mary, the Mother of God. Mary who is like us in everything and who pondered these things in her heart.

If you go with Mary, take these mysteries one by one. Now there are twenty of them. Saint Pope John Paul II, as I am sure many of you know, added another set of decades to the rosary. Before we used to have the Joyful Mysteries that were about Jesus' birth; the Sorrowful Mysteries that were about his passion and death; and the Glorious Mysteries that were about his resurrection. Saint Pope John Paul II, certainly inspired by the Holy Spirit, said, well what about the middle part? What about his public ministry? And he gave us these five beautiful mysteries, the Luminous Mysteries of the Holy Rosary. If you think about what each one is, you will notice that each one is a little vignette where Mary was able to see, observe, and ponder something in her heart. To say the rosary is a way to go with Mary into that pondering and reflection. It is a way to take all of the things that Mary saw, one after another, and to ponder them in our hearts together with Mary. As we do that, there emerges, from our memory and in our present attention, all that Jesus has accomplished for us. We become more aware of the sort of world we live in.

What sort of a world do we live in? My friends, we cannot evaluate the world in which we live without realizing the work that Christ has done for us. We cannot forget that he has come, as we celebrate in today's feast. He has become one of us and has assimilated us to himself through our baptism. He has given us a share in his very life. And he has united us to his mission here on earth – which is the salvation of all.

The praying of the rosary is a beautiful way to recover a sense of reality. When someone makes an outlandish suggestion, we say, "Get real!" Right? I like that expression, "Get real!" My friends, there's no way to get real without Christ. We can't get real, we don't get real, without the memory and recognition of Christ. The memory of Christ means bearing Christ in mind. Without bearing Christ in mind, we don't get real. We actually get sucked down into a vortex of darkness. But this is no longer a world of darkness. As so many of the beautiful hymns that have been sung for us in this holy season of Christmas, we express a light that is real.

So, let us ask our Blessed Mother today that we might really, truly, and radically get real. That we might get real in recognizing the great event that we celebrate today.

January 1, 2016
The Octave Day of Christmas
Solemnity of the Blessed Virgin Mary, the Mother of God

READINGS

First Reading: Numbers 6:22-27
Second Reading: Galatians 4:4-7
Gospel Reading: Luke 2:16-21

COLLECT

O God, who through the fruitful virginity of Blessed Mary bestowed on the human race the grace of eternal salvation, grant, we pray, that we may experience the intercession of her, through whom we were found worthy to receive the author of life, our Lord Jesus Christ, your Son. Who lives and reigns with you in the unity of the Holy Spirit, one God, for ever and ever.

Bearing the Life of Divinity

We truly rejoice today in this feast of Mary the Mother of God. We rejoice in this title because it reaffirms the greatness, the wonder, the splendor, and dimension of the extraordinary gift that we have in our Christian faith. This title also reaffirms the nature of our baptismal life and what exactly that life is.

There was a time, 1700 years ago, when the issue of whether or not Mary deserved this title was as big an issue as some of today's issues, maybe similar to the issue of gay marriage or abortion. This title of Mary's was what everyone was talking about. Everyone was concerned about whether or not Mary really deserved this title the Mother of God. Was this really an appropriate title for Mary? There were some who said, no, Mary shouldn't be called the Mother of God— that's too much, too excessive. Some decided that it's better just to say that Mary was the Mother of the humanity of Jesus.

The biggest problem with making that distinction, as understood by the Fathers of the Church who lived the faith, was that it removed Christ from us. Those who were living the faith most intensely and who were most contemplative of the mysteries of the faith knew it would have made of our Christianity, rather than the extraordinary adventure in history of the companionship of God with man, just one more call to observance. If Mary was only the mother of Jesus' humanity, our religion would be just one more call to put our life in order by ourselves in response to the will of God. But no, the Fathers of the Church, Saint Athanasius and his friends, insisted that the baby who was born of Mary was not a divided person. They insisted that the baby born of Mary was not a human person that just happened to have divinity tagged on, as something added. Instead, there was an intimate, total, and complete union in his person of those two natures. Therefore, that baby that Mary bore in her womb, and whose birth we're celebrating in these days, was God. And Mary, being the one who bore him in her womb, and gave birth to him, is the Mother of God.

The affirmation that this feast celebrates is not primarily about Mary, it's about Christ. The affirmation is about the life that we have received and what Christianity is. It goes to the very core and nature of what Christianity is— so much so that this morning as we consider the feast of Mary, Mother of God, we can rejoice again in gladness at what it is that has happened to us. We can rejoice at what this history, what this human reality bears with it and that we are part of it. We can rejoice that our Christianity isn't just another religion or an attempt to in some way respond to the evidently present and existent God who's a mysterious unknown. Instead we rejoice that we belong to the companionship of God. We are indeed the sons and daughters of the Father, the brothers and sisters of Jesus.

Therefore, we bear with us a real participation in the divine life of God. It is so great and so beautiful a gift, that time and time again the temptation to diminish it exists because it is almost too great and too beautiful a gift. Right? We feel like Peter who said, "Depart from me for I am a sinful man" (Luke 5:8) when he saw Jesus revealed in the fullness of his divinity. He had an instinctive reaction to want to back away. Again and again in history, this will to retreat and attempt to diminish the gift that we have received in Christ reasserts itself.

Well, this crisis in the life of the Church that was resolved at the Council of Ephesus was just one of those moments when some Christians said that the gift we have received in Christ is too much, and let's just be religious people. By religious people, they meant let's just strive to be honorable and to stand in the best possible relationship we can with God. Certainly, we do all of that. But in actual fact we are a people who bear God's presence. We are a people who bear God with us and in whom God has chosen to dwell and live. Becoming one of us, God has chosen to give us a participation in his very life. And everything that Jesus did was done not only by God, but truly by one of us also. Everything, all of the salvific work of God, of Jesus, was done by Jesus of Nazareth – truly man and truly God. To diminish or separate either of these two dimensions of Jesus is to undermine the very roots of the faith. It attempts to turn it back, as I say, into a re-proposal of an attempt, an inspired attempt, to be good. This would propose itself again and again throughout history in different forms. However, the experience and life of the Church, under the guidance of the Holy Spirit, would always manage to judge this re-proposal and say, "No. This is not what we are."

In fact, this method of judging is the way the doctrines of the Church always emerge. We can see this dynamic at work in our daily lives. You have probably not told anyone you love your mother recently because you have no reason to tell them. However, if I challenge you by saying that you don't love your mother, then you would say, "Yes, I do." The moment someone denies your love, that is the moment you have to affirm it, right? And that is the way the doctrines of the Church usually emerge because they only get stated in their full clarity when somebody puts them into question. In the meantime, the doctrines get carried along in the life of the Church. They are borne in the life of the Church in what we call the Tradition, with a capital T. One of the loci of the deposit of faith.

So, we rejoice today in this Motherhood of Mary. We rejoice with her, not just because of her greatness but because of the life, which through her has been given to us also. We who have been baptized have in some way been given that very same life that Mary was given from the first moment of her conception. We have been given this life precisely because Jesus was not two persons, but one person. Therefore, that life which we receive from him is his life, and it includes the life of the divinity.

As we celebrate our Mass, let us ask that we might rejoice in this life, and that we might become, during this year, ever more aware of that life which we bring to the world. This is the Year of Mercy.[2] Becoming aware of this divine life is one of the ways of understanding what it is to have a year of mercy. As I have pointed out many times, mercy is a divine attribute. And really, the only one who can truly be merciful is the one who can create. Mercy involves the covering of a deficit – a deficit of being. Therefore, only the creator can make up that deficit. To live the Year of Mercy is to live a year in which we grow in our awareness of the extraordinary gift which Christ gave to us once but also is giving to us continually and always. The fact that mercy lives in our community is a sure and certain sign of the fact that God himself, the Creator, also dwells among us. Let us ask for this awareness as we begin this year on the calendar. God bless you all.

---

[2] A Roman Catholic period of prayer held from the feast of the Immaculate Conception in 2015 to the Feast of Christ the King in 2016.

January 4, 2015
The Epiphany of the Lord

READINGS

First Reading: Isaiah 60:1-6
Second Reading: Ephesians 3:2-3A, 5-6
Gospel Reading: Matthew 2:1-12

COLLECT

O God, who on this day revealed your only begotten son to the nations by the guidance of a star, grant, in your mercy, that we, who already know you by faith, may be brought to behold the beauty of your sublime glory.

Changing the Equation

I remember some years ago, after September 11th, in that difficult moment in our country's history, one of the phrases you heard discussed in politics was "changing the equation." I don't know if you remember hearing that, "We've got to do something to change the equation." We did not like the equation; we did not like the solution coming from the equation, so we wanted to change it. So, we sent forth our young men to fight. We dropped our bombs and we did all those things that we thought might help to change the equation. I don't know if bombs will ever really change the equation in the long term. However, today's Feast of the Epiphany is precisely the confirmation that the equation has radically been changed for everyone in the world. You know that history has two dimensions, right? It has time and it has space. For example, if you want to identify an event in history, you might say, "In Dublin, in 1527." You have identified the event in two coordinates, time and space. Today's great Feast of the Epiphany reaches every time and every space. We are celebrating a truly universal fact that the equation has been radically changed.

The ultimate meaning of this Feast of the Epiphany, for every human being who lives in every time and in every space, is that the old equation no longer applies. The old equation, for which you can find no good solution, has been radically changed. I do not mean the geopolitical situation in the world, in 2011 or in any other year.

What I mean is the equation in which we seek to resolve the deepest needs of our own hearts. That equation that is our life for which we can find no adequate solution in this world.

Well, today's feast is the proclamation that once and forever, that equation is changed. Now there is a good route and a good value that solves that equation. And that value is none other than this child whose birth we are celebrating in this holy Christmas season. He really and truly changes the equation for us. He changes the equation of the human heart. The human heart's equation, before Jesus came, was an equation that only had bad solutions. Today that equation has one great and good solution, which is life in Jesus Christ our savior and communion with our heavenly Father, through Jesus. This is the positive solution to the equation that the Lord has given us.

Let's go back for a moment to those three kings. Those three wise men, those three magi have many, many names, but we do not quite understand from any of the names exactly who they were. I think, having considered it, that probably the closest people to whom we could compare them today are scientists. We hear every day about what scientists are saying about our world. We all know that if scientists say it, it is serious stuff, right? Well, these three kings were men of intelligence. These three magi were men who sought to understand and puzzle out everything to find its solution. They wanted to understand what reality is about. Perhaps we would say they are scientists with a little bit of philosopher thrown in. They were philosophers and scientists who were seekers of truth and meaning. These three wise men were indeed people who knew that the human equation did not have a good solution. Therefore, they were always on the lookout. They were always scanning the horizon of their lives to see if there was any hint or sign of something that could change that equation. These men were searching for something that would provide the possibility of a truly and really good outcome to this thing that we call life. Is there a solution that can provide a really and truly good outcome for life? These three kings were looking for this. This is what they wanted. This is what they sought.

One day that extraordinary star appeared in the sky, and that was something deeply puzzling to these men. The star was something completely new and attractive. It was something that drew them. They became curious about it, and they wanted to know more. So, they began to follow that star. They left their homeland and all the good things that they had known at home. They traveled the long, long distance not knowing where it would end or if they were only halfway there. They traveled without knowing where their destiny was. But they kept going.

Around this time last year, I published a poem by T.S. Eliot in the bulletin. The poem was called *The Journey of the Magi,*[3] and in it there was a beautiful reflection on this event. It was not an easy journey and there were many occasions on which you could have seen it was better to turn back, not to bother any more, or maybe it was better to settle for a while in this or that village. After all, these wise men were living in a time

---

[3] Eliot, T.S., *Ariel Poems* (London: Faber and Faber, 1927)

not too long after the nomadic ages, so they could easily settle in one village or another. But they kept going. They kept persevering. They kept following that star. They kept seeking what it was that the star promised until they arrived in Jerusalem.

Tonight we heard the story in the Gospel about their arrival in Jerusalem. We heard about the way their arrival scared King Herod, who loved his power and did not want any stars coming along and changing his formula. For Herod the formula was working. He wasn't thinking about a good outcome to life, he was thinking about his pleasures, his power, and all the sycophants that he had around him. For Herod, that was OK. Herod was willing to settle for that. That was all he wanted. He did not want anything new to happen. He did not want a new beautiful star appearing on the horizon and drawing the attention away from him. It is a story that we all know.

Now let us see if we can find a parallel and learn something from these wise men. The opening prayer of this mass implies that there is still a journey to be made. There's still a journey going on and we are not at the final end yet. Let's read the prayer one more time.

> O God, who on this day revealed your only begotten son to the nations by the guidance of a star, grant, in your mercy, that we, who already know you by faith, may be brought to behold the beauty of your sublime glory.

Here we see the part of the journey that remains. We know Jesus. We know Him by faith, we know him through the life of grace that we live in the Church. Yet we want to come to that place where he is all in all. We want to come to that place where everything is his, and everything belongs to Him. We want to see Him in the fullness of his glory. So, there is a journey for us too. What we can learn from those wise men is that we too must set out on a journey. We can't just tread water in life. We need, at a certain point, and the sooner the better, to set out on the real journey of life. This journey is towards our destiny in Christ. Now, as our star, we have Christ. Christ himself is the light of the world. We have the greatest star that there could be. We have the person of Christ, who in a few moments will give himself to us in the Eucharist. We have Him who animates the body which is the Church, and the Church that guides us and points the way. Just like those magi, there will be times when it seems that it would be better to turn back. There will be times when it seems better to give up or just to stop for a while to take a break from the journey of life. But we need to learn from the magi to continue to persevere, to follow, and to seek. When we get confused and we feel lost, we need to continue to seek out and try to rediscover the way.

What did the magi do when the star disappeared? They asked those who they thought would know. Here also is an important lesson for us. When we think we have lost the way, what do we do? Do we just give up? Or do we ask? Do we ask the Church? Do we call up the priest? For example, we can say, "Father, there's something going on in my life that's got me a little bit off track and I'd like to come and talk to you." Or maybe just go to confession and talk there. The Church exists for that; so that each one of us may be able to faithfully make the journey towards the fullness of life in Christ.

The Church exists so that each of us may be able to end up in the heavenly Jerusalem. Jerusalem, in all of the scriptures, and for all of the fathers of the Church, came to represent the kingdom of heaven. The heavenly Jerusalem. So, as the magi were destined to the terrestrial Jerusalem, we are destined to the heavenly Jerusalem. We are destined to the definitive encounter with Christ. The heavenly Jerusalem is where what we ask for in that opening prayer of the Mass will be fulfilled. Let us be ready this year, then, for a journey.

The deacon read for us the proclamation of the feasts; it is not just a formality but again shows us that there is a road. We will be accompanied on that road as we make a journey of faithfulness. A liturgical journey in which we will walk in the companionship of Christ, following the star of his presence here and now in the Church. We are being led faithfully to come and pay him homage in the fullness of life in his heavenly kingdom.

Let us ask for the grace of courage to make this journey this year, and in the coming years, with a star for each and every one of us.

January 5, 2015
Memorial of St. John Neumann

READINGS

First Reading: 1 John 3:22-4:6
Gospel Reading: Matthew 4:12-17, 23-25

COLLECT

O God, who called the Bishop Saint John Neumann, renowned for his charity and pastoral service, to shepherd your people in America, grant by his intercession that, as we foster the Christian education of youth and are strengthened by the witness of brotherly love, we may constantly increase the family of your Church. Through our Lord Jesus Christ, your Son, who lives and reigns with you in the unity of the Holy Spirit, one God, for ever and ever.

Enduring Gladness

When you come down route 70 from the mountains toward Denver, at a certain point there's a big sign that says, "Don't be fooled. You're not down yet. 4 more miles of steep downhill." Well, it would be good to have a sign like that today, because so many people think that once the Epiphany is over, it is all done. But it is absolutely not done. There is one precious week of Christmas time left, and in this week we get a chance to reflect more deeply on the great event that has occurred in the world, which is the birth of Christ.

The Feast of the Epiphany allows us to begin to really consider all of the implications of the fact that God has come into the world. Instead of focusing on the little baby in the manger, though we do still remember him, the focus now is on the event itself. We focus on the great event and all that comes to us through the birth of our savior into the world.

Today's Gospel gives us another moment of Christ's manifestation into the world; his mission in Galilee. We remember Jesus' mission to the towns and villages when we say the third mystery, the Luminous Mysteries, in the Holy Rosary. The third mystery is the announcement of the kingdom of heaven. "Repent, for the kingdom of heaven is at hand," Jesus says. That is the summary of his preaching in this northern Galilean ministry. The kingdom of heaven is at hand and has been given to us.

In the opening prayer of today's Mass, we heard about the gift of enduring gladness. And this is a beautiful consideration. A beautiful way to think for a moment about what Christ has brought to us. Yesterday in the homily I spoke about Christ as the only one who really changes the equation. The only one who really changes the outcome of the human condition. One of the ways to consider this change that Jesus brings is what that prayer and the liturgy calls *enduring gladness*. Gladness is the deepest, most complete, and most perfect happiness. Happiness sometimes simply means a smiling face. It is something passing, right? Like an emoji that you get in your email. Happiness is just a little smiley face, while gladness goes to the very root of what happiness is; the very source of happiness. Gladness goes to the piece of soul, to the encounter of the soul, to what truly corresponds to the soul. In other words, gladness is the adherence of the person to that for which they are made. In that encounter with the one for whom we are made, God made visible, in the humanity of Christ, we are finally, truly, really and completely at peace. And that peace allows us to say, even if the circumstances are what we traditionally call bad, that really, we are truly OK. Everything is truly well and good. The absolute ultimate positivity of everything comes from Jesus. This positivity is impossible without Jesus. In the encounter with Jesus we truly live this experience of peace in the heart.

I have often told you about that little Pieta book I found on the floor in the Church after we celebrated Mass for cancer victims. When I looked inside the front cover, I saw someone had written in old-fashioned handwriting, "Thy will be done

Lord." I kept the little book and the next week I asked if anyone dropped it. It turned out that the book belonged to a lady who never returned to Mass because she died a couple of weeks later. She was in the hospital by the time I asked about the lost book. Those words that she was able to write, in the midst of her suffering, in the midst of her illness, facing the final journey across the threshold of death, were gladness. She was able to write, confidently and trustingly, not my will but *thy will be done*. That's the gladness that Jesus brings. This gift is something that comes from him alone. If we need and want that gladness, all we need do is draw closer to him. If we desire that gladness, all we need do is pay closer attention to him in our lives. Let Jesus truly be the center of our lives.

So, as we celebrate this Mass and as we continue the celebration of the Christmas season, let us ask Christ for this great gift of enduring gladness.

January 7, 2015
Wednesday after Epiphany

READINGS

First Reading: 1 John 4:11-18
Gospel Reading: Mark 6:45-52

COLLECT

O God, who adorned the Priest Saint Raymond with the virtue of outstanding mercy and compassion for sinners and for captives, grant us, through his intercession, that, released from slavery to sin, we may carry out in freedom of spirit what is pleasing to you. Through our Lord Jesus Christ, your Son, who lives and reigns with you in the unity of the Holy Spirit, one God, for ever and ever.

Epiphany Miracles

Today's readings show us these extraordinary examples of the manifestation of God's presence in the world. When people saw Jesus, they saw a man. They saw the characteristics of a man, and they recognized that Jesus was a man. But those who paid attention to him, those who saw him and watched him, noticed also a whole other set of things that were happening. They noticed that the actions emerging from Jesus couldn't simply be ascribed to his humanity. These signs are the focus of our meditation this week.

The Feast of the Epiphany, in its most ancient form, celebrates three great events. First, it celebrates the coming of the kings, which is the one event that we hold as central in the liturgy today. This feast also celebrates a second event, the wedding feast at Cana in Galilee. The third event celebrates in the Feast of the Epiphany is the baptism of Jesus in the Jordan, when the voice from heaven acknowledges Jesus as Lord. This week we celebrate the second and third miracles.

Miracle after miracle after miracle. Miracles worked by Jesus and not by strange machinations. Miracles Jesus worked by a simple gesture of his will. All he needed to do was decide and those miracles happened. These are manifestations of his divinity. Indeed, if you were to strip out of the Gospel all of the miracles of Jesus, you would find that the Gospel would become very tenuous. People who have the attitude that Jesus was only a man approach the Gospel with the opinion that the miracles could not happen. Those people never encounter

Jesus. They never recognize the true figure of Jesus himself. The miracles are a vital part of the way Jesus communicates. They give evidence to those who watch him, so that they can draw close to him and thereby come to discover more deeply the great mystery of his divinity.

So, we should never discard these miracles. They are part of the way in which Jesus came to reveal himself to us. We receive them as testimony in the Gospels and as events that happened to open the hearts of men to a deeper understanding and relationship with Jesus. Miracles were an essential part of coming to know Jesus. A miracle is a sovereign gesture of God. It's something that only God can do. It is a very simple logic for us and it was a very simple logic for the people of Israel. God made the laws of nature, and therefore if the normal laws of nature are suspended, then the one who is suspending them is at least very closely connected with the one who made them. Maybe you can think of when you see a police car flying down the road at 80 miles an hour. You don't think the police officer should get a speeding ticket. Instead you think that he must be connected in some way with the legal institutions that provide the law. It is analogous to this. If there's somebody, who with a simple gesture of his will can suspend the laws of nature, then that person must be connected in a very special way with the author of the laws of nature. Through miracles the people came to pay attention and to watch Jesus.

The miracles didn't always find in the people an open heart. Even for the apostles, Jesus' miracles were not always understood. This miracle of Jesus walking on the water happens immediately after the miracle of the multiplication of the loaves and the feeding of the five thousand. "They had not understood the incident of the loaves, on the contrary their hearts were hardened." (Mark 6:52) What does it mean that their hearts were hardened? It means that they ultimately resisted that openness of reason that the miracles were given to bring about. The miracles were brought about to allow us to open our reason and to listen and pay attention to Jesus. Miracles aren't ultimately a guarantee of faith. Miracles are given as a possibility and a provocation to open reason. So, when it says that their hearts were hardened, it means that instead of saying, "Wow. This is amazing! This is incredible. We really have to pay attention here," they closed their hearts. Instead of opening their reason, they closed it to him.

Jesus offers them another extraordinary miracle. It almost seems to happen by chance. It's as if Jesus is taking a short cut across the surface of the lake, and they happen to see him. When he gets into the boat, the storm is calmed. Jesus continually had with him this mastery over nature. It was absolutely a part of him.

We also have the case where Jesus cures Peter's sick mother-in-law. In this case it looks like a miracle of convenience. Jesus was there for dinner and Peter said his mother was sick, so Jesus made her better and she got up and made the dinner.

The Church offers us these miracles today because they are manifestations in the world of the presence of the divine. These miracles are manifestations of one who is divine; of God made man; of God-man. Jesus of Nazareth, true God and true man. Jesus was like us in everything but sin, as the Catechism teaches. But Jesus was also God from God, light from light, true God from true God. Jesus is both. He has both of these natures. And to those who spent time with him, his divine nature became visible through these signs. And that's the mystery of the Epiphany we celebrate during this week.

January 8, 2015
Thursday after Epiphany

READINGS

First Reading: 1 John 4:19-5:4
Gospel Reading: Luke 4:14-22

COLLECT

O God, who by the Nativity of your Only Begotten Son wondrously began for your people the work of redemption, grant, we pray, to your servants such firmness of faith, that by his guidance they may attain the glorious prize you have promised. Through our Lord Jesus Christ, your Son, who lives and reigns with you in the unity of the Holy Spirit, one God, for ever and ever.

Correspondence

It is clear in this Gospel how the Epiphany Feast theme continues with the manifestation of Jesus to the world. Here we have the revelation that in this man Jesus of Nazareth there dwells also another nature— the divine nature. In this case, Jesus makes this claim, but this claim meets a welcome ear in the people who are listening to it— at least in the first instance. Later on, they will react in different ways. In the most immediate hearing of his words the people find Jesus' revelation of a divine nature agreeable and consonant because they have begun to pay attention to him. They've begun to know him and perceive in him something that goes beyond the simple reality of being a good person. Jesus is more than a good person and a wonderful man. Jesus is more than a person with a great, powerful, and sweet temperament. There's also something mysterious there. Therefore, when Jesus applies this great Scripture about the Messiah to himself, immediately the people say, "Oh, okay." Their most immediate human reaction is to acknowledge and accept what Jesus says about himself. Then of course the drama will play out politically, because there are some people in Israel who have to respond to this. We know how the story will end with Jesus' crucifixion on the cross. But the first response to his claim is a response that recognizes the reasonableness of it. All were speaking highly of him and were amazed by the gracious words that came from his mouth.

What makes words gracious and amazing? Think about it. When do you hear a homily and you go out saying that it was a great homily? What is the ultimate ingredient that makes something pleasing to us? I would say that is its truth. What makes words gracious is the recognition that what is being said is the truth. The recognition that what is said is amazing, emerges from my hunger and yearning for truth. To describe this, Father Giussani uses the word *correspondence* to mean that the words Jesus spoke were fitting. Jesus' words reached something very deep in the human soul that perhaps we can never adequately put into words but yet is continually there. Jesus' words corresponded to that yearning and hunger for a relationship with God.

As they listened to Jesus, the people felt that they were reached in a way that was deeper than any other way. This is the way Jesus came to the world. He came to the world betting on that response of the human heart. And that is the Church's voice is as well. The Church doesn't play games with us. The Church addresses, as Jesus did, directly and unmediated, the deepest yearning and need of our heart. By addressing that, the Word of Christ finds a welcome witness. If we are simple and pure in heart, then what comes later in today's Gospel will not happen to us. That initial positive response of the people that the word of Jesus provokes will become the definitive word. His word will become verified as we live more and more and as we hear him more and more. As we welcome his great claim of divinity, we will become ever more secure and more certain.

As I said, the Church never plays games. That is why, for example, when I hear about these chastity programs, I am sometimes concerned. Instead of going to the heart of what chastity is about, which in a brief word is the truth of love, these programs sometimes start putting up PowerPoint slides about all the diseases and all the bad consequences that can come from promiscuity. That is not the way the Church speaks, and that's not the way that Christ speaks. Christ doesn't sell us a partial good, he sells us *the* good. What it they find a cure for all those bad diseases? Does that mean promiscuity is alright? If they find ways around the negative consequences of bad behavior, does that mean that the bad behavior becomes OK? Absolutely not. That is why the proposal of the Church isn't to try and control our behavior, by some partial goods. The voice of the Church is like the voice of Christ, it speaks to the very core of the human being. It says that in the case of chastity, the love between human beings is not something that we invent. It's not something small. It is a very participation in the life of God. The Church leads us through that understanding. The Church leads us to understand ever more deeply the vocation of the human being to love. It leads us to the rules of chastity that are simply the description of that faithful relationship of love. So it is with any area of life in the Church. The Church always speaks to the heart because the Church is the voice of Christ. Just as Christ, speaking to the hearts of these people, won their consent, the Church will win its deepest consent from us human beings by speaking to our hearts.

Let us ask as we celebrate the Holy Mass that we may be awake in heart and that our spirits may be awake and ready to recognize that which is true. If this is the case, truly nothing will separate us from the love of Christ.

January 9, 2016
The Baptism of Our Lord

READINGS

First Reading: Isaiah 42:1-4, 6-7
Second Reading: Acts 10:34-38
Gospel Reading: Luke 3:15-16, 21-22

COLLECT

Almighty ever-living God, who were pleased to shine forth with new light through the coming of your Only Begotten Son, grant, we pray, that, just as he was pleased to share our bodily form through the childbearing of the Virgin Mary, so we, too, may one day merit to become companions in his kingdom of grace. Who lives and reigns with you in the unity of the Holy Spirit, one God, for ever and ever.

Baptism into a Shared Life

This Feast of Jesus' Baptism at the Jordan is one of the great feasts. This feast not only concludes the Christmas season, but is an integral part of the Christmas celebration of the event of the coming of Our Lord into the world.

This great miracle of Jesus' baptism in the Jordan manifests the fullness of the Holy Trinity. It manifests the Father, whose voice speaks from heaven; the Holy Spirit, who comes upon Jesus in the form of the dove; and Jesus himself, who receives from the Father this sign of affirmation of his love and affection. This miracle reveals the Trinity to us and the life that Jesus has come to bring to the world. It is also a revelation of the life that Jesus has come to offer us. He comes to offer us a true and real participation by his very presence, by his brotherhood with us in the human condition. Jesus already establishes us in an extraordinary new dignity, as in some real sense brothers and sisters of our God. Then, through the mysterious gift of the sacrament of baptism, he incorporates us into a share in the divine life. This is the dignity that the Christian carries.

Saint Thomas Aquinas would tell us that we who have received this baptism are in actual fact something more as creatures than those who have not received this gift. There is an ontological change. We become more than what we were in our natural state.

Jesus came to bring us this new life, which is communicated to us through our baptism. All of our Christian faith has this as its core. This baptism comes to us not as a theoretical framework, but as the very depths of what's happening in the Christian life. In our baptism and in our life in Christ this great mystery is revealed. It is revealed in the way that we live our life, in the sacramental reality of our life, and in our life of journey and unity. All of this great mystery which is taking place in the Church is revealed in this feast today.

Jesus came to offer us this baptismal share in his divine life. He came of the unmotivated initiative of God to bring his love to the world. Not because he had to. One of the questions that is often posed about Jesus' baptism is why did Jesus have to be baptized? Well, Jesus didn't have to be baptized. Why did Jesus have to come into the world at all? He didn't have to come into the world at all. Why did Jesus have to die upon the cross? He didn't have to die on the cross at all. All of these things are the manifestation of him. They are his self-manifestation to us, and in all of these mysteries of our faith he communicates to us who God is and what God is like.

What sort of a God is our God? God by his very nature is mysterious to us, simply because we can't conceptualize him. Yet in the encounter with Christ, in the journey with Christ we come to know our God. In the coming of Christ to the world and in the life he gives us in baptism, we learn about our God. In the people Jesus met then, and in the people he meets now, in us, we walk in communion with our God. We know our God. Not conceptually, though. We can know things about God, but we can never know God conceptually. We can never entirely wrap our minds around God in such way that we "understand" him. He will always remain a mystery beyond the grasp of our intellect. However, the fascinating thing is that through Jesus we do know God. We are indeed the brothers of our God. We are the friends of God. This is the extraordinary mystery of our faith, which we can never completely ponder and which we can never completely understand. The mystery of our faith must, my brothers and sisters, leave us in awe and wonder as we consider what God has done for us.

Saint Pope John Paul II loved to reflect on the goodness of God for us. He used to love to meditate on this verse from the Psalms, "What is man that you should care for him." (Psalm 8:5) What are we that he should care for us so much, my brothers and sisters? That is not a question of philosophical inquiry. It is a question to focus our gaze on a revelation. This is the way John Paul II loved to contemplate the human condition. He always started from the incarnation of Christ, which is ultimately the only place in which you can adequately contemplate the human condition. My friends, we are so precious that God sent his son to us. We are so precious that Jesus has come to us. We are so precious that Jesus entered the human condition in everything except sin. In his baptism in the Jordan we already see a prefiguring of his death upon the cross because it reveals to us the totality, the completeness of his embrace of our condition. Jesus entering the human condition shows that he is going to truly walk with us as our brother. Jesus is going to share this human condition of ours in every single way. He is not going to be foreign to any of the experiences that we have as human beings except in that tragic experience which is the use of our own will to separate ourselves, to take a distance, and to stand away from God. Jesus will experience our condition in every way except in the denial of our very self. He won't share in that condition which is our destruction. Yet in all else he comes to share his life with us. The fullness of his life with us.

As Jesus reveals himself in the blessed Trinity, we come to know more profoundly and more deeply who God is. We come to know God in relationship and as relationship. Father, Son, and Holy Spirit. This deep mystery will be meditated on throughout Christian history. Found in the writings of the New Testament, pondered upon by the fathers of the Church, and clarified throughout the centuries we find meditations on this deeply mysterious relationship. The great doctrines of our faith are defined and clarified in the life and the experience of the Church under the guidance of the Holy Spirit.

We come to know who God is in relationship. In actual fact, when we read in the Scriptures, when we read John and Paul saying to us that God is love, already here we begin to intuit the fact that if God is love, in some way relationship must be at the very core of the divine nature. The philosophers used to say that all of reality is good, true, and beautiful. These properties Aristotle called the transcendentals, or the realities that the mind can perceive in every single being. God reveals to us a property that we could consider another transcendental: this openness to and need for relationship. This fulfillment can be found only in relationship. It is a characteristic of our God, of the Supreme Being himself. And therefore, it brings us beyond the conquests of the great philosophical tradition and allows us to understand the mystery of love. Relationship helps us understand why we as a Christian people are community. It helps us understand why baptism is an entrance into a common life, a shared life, a communion of life. We are invited to share in that divine life and without that dimension of our life we are truly poor. That dimension which is the capacity to say "You" to another. That relationship is revealed in its true identity which is love. The true and great love. The love of *agape*. The love that God has revealed, and that is ultimately revealed most dramatically, and most fully for us in his holy cross.

I know that is a lot to think about. These are simply some thoughts that can accompany us as we celebrate this mystery of the baptism of the Lord. This is one of those feasts that risks being overlooked in its significance and importance. Today I wanted to point out just how much we have invested in the extraordinary event that we celebrate today. In the Eastern Church it stands as one of the highest feasts and indeed in our Church also. So as we celebrate this Mass and as we stand now professing our faith in the Trinity, let us ask our Lord that we might welcome evermore truly and freely in our hearts that Trinitarian life which he offers to us and thank him for the gift he has given to us in baptism.

January 10, 2015

READINGS

First Reading: 1 John 5:14-21
Gospel Reading: John 3:22-30

COLLECT

Almighty ever-living God, who were pleased to shine forth with new light through the coming of your Only Begotten Son, grant, we pray, that, just as he was pleased to share our bodily form through the childbearing of the Virgin Mary, so we, too, may one day merit to become companions in his kingdom of grace. Who lives and reigns with you in the unity of the Holy Spirit, one God, for ever and ever.

Vocation in Every Circumstance

John the Baptist testifies to Jesus that he accepts his vocation entirely and totally. John does not try to cling to anything or let his heart be attached to anything except the great vocation that the Lord has given him. John's call is to be the precursor to Christ. This issue of vocation is very, very important for us too. To each one of us, God has given a vocation. That vocation is defined principally by our circumstances in life, and it is in our "Yes" to our vocation that our "Yes" to God takes one of its most fundamental expressions. When we say "Yes" with all our heart to the vocation that God has given us, then we have set the scene for a truly great cooperation in the life of grace. It doesn't mean that there won't be struggles along the road. It doesn't mean that there won't be moments of weakness and even falls on the road; in that "Yes" to our vocation, we truly set up our lives in a way that gives us the real potential for holiness. We begin a cooperation with grace that in the fullness of time will lead to real holiness.

When we don't pay attention to our vocation, when we think for example, as a parent, that the more time I can get off from the care of my children the better, we lose our way. This is when we really close ourselves to that journey of holiness. If, instead of caring for our children we think that what we really want is to sit in front of the computer unbothered, we have lost our way. When our heart is divided and we think that in some sense the duties that come to us as part of our vocation are a hindrance to our happiness, this is when we really close ourselves to that journey of holiness that Christ offers to each one.

Holiness does not come to us human beings in an instant except in some extraordinary instances when God has wanted to do that. We can perhaps think of Maria Goretti or some of the early martyrs who, in their extreme youth, were able to perceive entirely and totally their belonging to God and prefer it. But for most of us, life is a journey of growth, of walking with God and toward God. And when we walk with God we are freed in time from all of those false attachments that sometimes hinder our hearts.

John the Baptist is a great example for us of the living out of the"Yes" to his vocation which defined his life and his mission. John the Baptist realizes that his greatness is the "Yes" to his vocation, and not in any personal claim. You know John the Baptist was very, very popular. If he just kind of blurred the edges a little bit on the idea about whether he was the Messiah or not, if John kind of demurred when he was asked the question, and kind of used some sort of subterfuge not to answer it directly, then people would have held him up. John could have had a huge following, but his vocation was clear to him, and he said "Yes" to it. John affirmed his vocation and he lived his life according to it.

Tomorrow we'll be back to the green robes and to ordinary time with all its beauties and its richness. On this last day of the Epiphany week, I propose to you that we ask the Lord for the grace of a profound and deep "Yes" to our vocation. We could say a lot of things about vocation, because vocation is what we might call a word that is analogous. In other words, it can be applied in many different ways, to many different degrees. For example, illness has a vocational element. When we are ill, if we have an illness, even if it's just the flu and it's going to pass in a week or two, that is still a vocation. We can think that this circumstance is against me, and God is not my friend because I'm sick. Sometimes that's the way we act, with hostility to reality. Every element in life, every circumstance in life in some way details the vocation that God has given us. In its most radical sense, the vocation that God gives us is a doorway to a possibility of a journey of grace. In the case of some, vocation is a life of consecration. In the case of others, it is a vocation to marriage, and the vocation to fatherhood, motherhood, and the spousal relationship. These are all circumstances to which that great "Yes" is a doorway to a possibility of a journey of grace.

I want to emphasize that living our vocation is something that enters into every moment of our lives, into every circumstance that we live. When Bishop Massimo, the founder of the Saint Charles Borromeo fraternity, spoke about circumstances, he would say that "If I shoot you, then I have to answer to God for shooting you. However, you have to live the vocation of being a person who was shot." Because that is your journey to holiness. Your journey to holiness is to live that circumstance in front of God and in relationship with God.

So, let us ask that in every aspect of life we may say "Yes" to our vocation. Let us ask courageously with Saint John the Baptist for our vocation, to honor Christ. Let us ask that we might also live our vocation with such clarity and such affirmation that we can resist the voices of the world that so often tell us that our happiness is elsewhere.

January 11, 2015
The Baptism of the Lord

READINGS

First Reading: Isaiah 55:1-1
Second Reading: 1 John 5:1-9
Gospel Reading: Mark 1:7-11

COLLECT

Almighty ever-living God, who, when Christ had been baptized in the River Jordan and as the Holy Spirit descended upon him, solemnly declared him your beloved Son, grant that your children by adoption, reborn of water and the Holy Spirit, may always be well pleasing to you. Through our Lord Jesus Christ, your Son, who lives and reigns with you in the unity of the Holy Spirit, one God, for ever and ever.

The Feast of Baptism

His baptism is the beginning of Jesus' public ministry. It is the definitive manifestation by God when Jesus is made known by the heavenly Father as the one in whom He is well pleased, his beloved son. Perhaps the best message we can take away from the celebration of this feast is to remember that we have been bathed in those same waters as Jesus of Nazareth. We too have been lowered into the river and baptized. In an analogous but a very real way, our heavenly Father has expressed over us through the graces of Jesus Christ the same judgment that he has expressed over his beloved son. Of us, he has made his sons and daughters and he is also well pleased in us. Consider that – he is pleased by us. The pleasure that God takes in us comes through our baptism. Our baptism has its force and its strength in the grace that was won for us by Jesus of Nazareth. This grace is given to us in baptism when we are united with him in water. Therefore, we too are configured in grace, and therefore we are pleasing to God.

It is often pointed out, especially when someone older is baptized, that at the moment of your baptism, when you come up from those waters, you are entirely justified, good, and without any stain or hint of sin. In fact, at that very moment, if you were to die you would go straight to heaven – no purgatory or anything else. After your baptism you would go straight to the presence of God. And that's precisely because in baptism we are made pleasing to God. So, our heavenly

Father says of each one of us that he is pleased, in a true way, not the same as for Jesus, but in a way that is analogous. The Church uses the word analogous to signify something whose nature is the same but whose degree is different. So, in a different degree our heavenly Father says over each one of us: this is my beloved son, or this is my beloved daughter. In him or in her I am well pleased. Our heavenly Father is pleased with us and the work that Jesus is doing in us.

After baptism comes the journey of life and the continual plague of sin, in which we opt out of that pleasure of God. In sinning we turn against God. Parents are probably very familiar with this behavior of turning away. The children that we love with all our hearts turn against us in certain moments. The children for whom we would do anything say nasty things, reject our authority, try to insult us, and disobey us. Children do all those sorts of things. And again, by analogy, in a differing degree, we too, in our relationship with our heavenly Father, in whose presence Jesus has made us pleasing, try to rebel against God. We turn away from him, we try to insult him, and we try to find other ways for living independently of him. Do you not think that the pain that you as a parent might feel, again in some analogous way, is the same pain that God feels? All of the suffering and sins of all the world were brought together in Jesus' crucifixion and death, and he bore them all by himself. By himself he won for us the grace of salvation.

Therefore, our baptism does not go away. God does not rescind our baptism. He has already faced and dealt with all of our sin. He has already, as we might say today, taken on board all of our sin. Instead of punishing us for our sin, his son suffers his passion for us. Continually the Lord offers us ways to return to him. Like the famous Rembrandt painting of the Prodigal Son, Jesus wants to leave us with an image. He leaves us with an image of the father of that prodigal son who waited, day and night, scanning the horizon, for our return. He still waits even today for the chance that we would be willing to return to the baptismal graces which were given to us and which he still honors.

Indeed, the problem isn't that God does not honor our baptismal graces, but that we don't. Although we don't always honor our baptismal graces, our baptismal dignity remains. God does not turn his back on his beloved but wants conversion and a change of heart and a coming to him.

Let us turn again, then, for a moment to the state we were in at the moment of our baptism. The state we were in when all that happened in our life was that we had encountered Christ. The state we were in when Christ paid the price of our sins and allowed us to be washed in that very same water in which he was washed. Let us return to the state when Jesus had made us pleasing to God. That's the life for which we are made. It is the right life for us, the healthy life, the good and appropriate life. Everything else is an aberration. Everything else is confusion, noise, distraction, and destruction.

The life that we are made for is that life of communion with God. To live that baptismal life daily is what we call holiness.

As you know, we can recover at any point that state of being pleasing to God. All we need to do is return to him and ask him for his mercy. If we've truly opted out of his pleasure by mortal sin, then we go to confession. By confessing our sins, it is he himself who gives us the grace of his passion so that we can be once again pleasing to the Father. If our sins are small and don't represent a breaking of the relationship, then we didn't truly leave our Father's house. Here again we can return to the story of the prodigal son. The prodigal son left his father's house. He decided that his father's house was not the place for him and that he would make his life elsewhere. That's how the Church understands mortal sin. Saint John the Evangelist spoke about it in the Gospel. If we haven't turned away or truly decided that we have a better plan for our happiness, then it's enough that we be present at Mass. If we haven't left our father's house, then it is enough that we make an act of contrition. Any act of love is enough to return us to our heavenly Father. When we return, we immediately perceive his loving gaze.

When we leave our Father's house, we have to come back. That is why the Church prescribes that we go to confession whenever we have committed a mortal sin. A mortal sin is a choice so grave, and so opposed to the will of the Father, that it really does represent a departure. It is a rejection of his delight in us. We are like the prodigal son in the painting who is completely disheveled, shoes worn out, with holes in his clothes. Now look at the father who embraces him. That is the sacrament of confession. The sacrament of confession is not a sacrament of reconciling an account, and it is not a military soldier reporting to his commander about a failed mission. The sacrament of confession is an invitation to return to the Father's house. The son tried to say, "Well, father, I am no longer worthy to be called your son, treat me as one of your hired servants." (Luke 15:19) We realize that we have betrayed our Father. But the father of the prodigal son, instead of listening to those words, embraces him and prepares for him the great feast of his return. Such a feast always awaits us when we return to our baptismal life.

This Feast of Baptism is the life of the Church. If you read the fullness of the liturgy, in all of its parts, you will see that it is a feast that celebrates the great gift of baptism. As the earliest Church fathers pointed out, when we are baptized, we receive baptismal graces through the sign of the water. However, when Jesus was baptized, the transfer went in the other direction. From him there went forth the graces that would forever after give power to the baptismal waters to assimilate us to the work of Christ and to the salvation which he has won for us.

As we say this Holy Mass, let us ask that we may truly journey as a baptismal people. Let us be a people pleasing to the Lord. And should we depart from him, let us ask that we may rapidly return to our baptismal life, and that we may always walk together as the community of his great family, the sons and daughters of his who live together in the pleasure of our Father. This really is paradise on earth. The trouble is we don't seem to be able to do it yet. But let us ask that each and every place where we are, in our homes, with our families, our community, that we may become ever more that communion of people, the sons and daughters of our heavenly Father, in whom he takes pleasure.

LENT & EASTER

February 10, 2016
Ash Wednesday

READINGS

First Reading: Joel 2:12-18
Second Reading: 2 Corinthians 5:20-6:2
Gospel Reading: Matthew 6:1-6, 16-18

COLLECT

Grant, O Lord, that we may begin with holy fasting this campaign of Christian service, so that, as we take up battle against spiritual evils, we may be armed with weapons of self-restraint. Through our Lord Jesus Christ, your Son, who lives and reigns with you in the unity of the Holy Spirit, one God, for ever and ever.

Return to Me with All Your Heart

A sin is truly a terrible thing. Sometimes we think that sin is sort of okay. But if we were to truly contemplate what a sin is, we would understand that it is truly unacceptable. We would understand that there really is no tragedy that can happen to us in life that is the equal of committing a sin. It used to be asked, would the complete works of William Shakespeare be well lost for the non-commission of one venial sin? The only correct answer to that question is, "Yes, they would be well lost." In other words, we would rather lose the complete works of William Shakespeare than commit one venial sin. Why do we have things like that in our tradition? Well, it's because of the ontology. It's because of the way reality is. Everything has its origin in God. Everything comes from God. That which is of God is good, beautiful, and true. That which is not of God is destructive, corrupt, broken, hurtful, and less. This is what sin is.

One of the first things we need to have in this Lenten season is the cultivation of a horror of sin. Would that we could never ever sin again. We would really and truly like to never be able to sin again. Unfortunately, that's probably not going to happen. Would that it would happen but it's probably not going to. When Christ blessed his Church with many, many gifts, one of the gifts was not superior moral standards. In actual fact, Christians are very much like every other people in terms of their morality. This is because Jesus didn't choose to give us some magic bypass on the journey of our freedom to say "Yes" to him. Adam and Eve were given the freedom to say "Yes" to God through that tree in the center of the Garden of Eden, and they chose to say "No" by eating the forbidden fruit. Each one of us has that same dignity and is endowed by God with freedom. To that freedom God makes an invitation to come to him, to be with him, to be united to him. He invites us to live our human condition entirely in him. Our freedom is given to us so that we can say "Yes" to this invitation of God. That is what our freedom is for. That's why Jesus didn't take away sin from us. To take away sin would not have been to redeem us, but rather to disfigure us, and indeed to destroy us. To do so would mean taking away his greatest gift, which is the possibility of having merit before God through our "Yes." To really participate in our belonging to God is that "Yes" that we say to him.

The first reading opened with the cry of the Lord through the prophet Joel. "Even now," says the Lord, "return to me with all your heart." The invitation of Jesus is always there. Always present and always renewed. "Return to me with all your heart." Don't go Adam's route. Don't go Eve's route. God is saying come to me. Come to me and stay with me. Use that freedom with which I created you for the purpose for which I created it, so that you could be with me forever in freedom. Do not use it to destroy and disfigure and hurt and harm yourself. Above all do not use it to say that ultimate "No" to me. That "No" would cast us out of his life forever because God will not compel our reason.

This Lenten journey has this invitation of Jesus at its core, an invitation that we all wish to accept. You wouldn't all be gathered here around this altar today, in the middle of the day, on a busy day of the week, Ash Wednesday, if we didn't want to answer "Yes" to Christ. You wouldn't be here if you didn't want to answer "Yes" to God's invitation. Even now God is saying "return to me with all your heart." There is not one of us here gathered around this altar today that does not desire in the very depths of our heart to say "Yes" to Christ. Yet somehow, we are burdened with the fact that we know when we go out there today, tomorrow, the next day, and the weeks and months to come, that in so many little ways we will continue to say our "No" to him. Our Lenten journey is an opportunity and an invitation. It's an opportunity that the Church gives us as a people gathered together to beg the Lord and to ask for the special grace of truly being able to say "Yes" to Christ. You have to understand that discipline is not at the center of this Lenten season. Lent isn't a gloomy season of purple vestments, gloomy thoughts, sacrifice, penance, and fasting. No, no, no, no, no. This is a season in which our hearts are invited to soar!

Holy people everywhere long for the season of Lent because they know what a treasure and a beauty it is. The testimony of the saints speaks of this over and over again. Remember, my friends, you and I are called to be saints. You and I are called to enjoy this season. Not with the enjoyment of self-indulgence but with the enjoyment of a heart that finally finds its place. With the enjoyment of a heart that finally does what the heart most truly and dearly desires to do.

Jesus introduces us to the three great practices of Lent in this Gospel. Did you know that Lent and the practice of Lent are based on this Gospel reading? It's interesting the way Jesus says it. He doesn't say "Don't look for fame, because you won't get it." He doesn't say "Don't look for praise and admiration by the people when they see the intensity of your prayers, because you won't get it." He doesn't say "Don't give alms publicly, so that you are esteemed, because you won't get esteem." He tells us you will get those things. If that's what you want, you will get it. If what you want is fame, you'll get it. If what you want is esteem and honor, you'll get it. If what you want is people to look at you and say, "Oh, what a marvelous person so and so is," you'll get that. But my friends, how low we have set the standards. How low we have set the goal of our heart if all we want is a little bit of human praise. Jesus' invitation isn't to want less, but to want more. To want something greater and better. Indeed, Jesus' invitation is to want something infinitely good, which is communion and life with him. That is why Jesus invites us to engage in these practices with purity of heart. Seeking anything less than the love of God, for which our hearts were made, means our hearts cannot be satisfied.

If you think Lent would be better with banquets every single day in which we can gorge on the pleasures of this world, then do that. If you think Lent would be better by holding everything we possibly can for ourselves and making a few great killings in the stock market, then do that. If you think it would be better to be seen as a great hero of our time, then do that. But my friends, I think you and I know that there is a pearl of greater price. There is a pearl of greater price to be found here. And this is what Lent is about. Lent is about choosing, preferring, and deciding that what we want is that pearl of great price which Jesus used as an illustration, a metaphor for his life and his love.

My friends, let us ask as we celebrate and begin our holy Lenten journey that we may be truly guided through this Lenten season. Let us be guided not by some sort of a feeling or need for self-flagellation, but rather by a great desire of heart to truly be free of all the entrapments that distract us. Let us ask that we might be given the grace to adhere. Let us pray that we might have God. You alone, O Lord, you alone. As they write over the main entrance to the great Benedictine monasteries, "You alone, O Lord." You alone and none other. Let us ask for that because as Jesus tells us, when we have that, everything else is given to us.

We are going to distribute the ashes now. The ashes are a symbol that remind us that life has a task. They remind us that this life isn't just a period time that is mostly on the level. Tomorrow will be more or less the same as today, so it would be easy to think we should just eat, drink, and be merry for tomorrow we die. No, my friends, let us find in this symbol of the ashes a greater spur to that prayer which I just expressed, the prayer of the desire for him and for him alone.

February 13, 2016
First Sunday of Lent

READINGS

First Reading: Deuteronomy 26:4-10
Second Reading: Romans 10:8-13
Gospel Reading: Luke 4:1-13

COLLECT

Almighty ever-living God look with compassion on our weakness and ensure us your protection by stretching forth the right hand of your majesty. Through our Lord Jesus Christ, your Son, who lives and reigns with you in the unity of the Holy Spirit, one God, for ever and ever.

The Temptation to Bypass Freedom

> What is man that you should care for him? The son of man that you should keep him in mind?

This is what the eighth psalm tells us. As we hear the readings for today, perhaps we can get a glimpse of what it is that Jesus is pursuing when he comes into the world. We can begin to get an idea of why such an extraordinary thing—Jesus coming into the world—would take place, and the sacrifice which he is about to complete for our salvation. These temptations of Jesus were real temptations, not just some sort of figurative language. Jesus desired to share our condition in every single way. The only thing in which Jesus didn't share in was the experience of actually choosing to sin. All of the fascination, all of the attractiveness, and all of the temptation that we human beings have to suffer, he also chose to suffer. Jesus wanted to know our condition and to share our condition completely, totally, and fully, with one exception: he would not share in that destructive behavior which is sin.

These temptations present to Jesus a possibility of trying to accomplish his mission while in some way avoiding human freedom. This freedom to choose is the mysterious and extraordinary thing that you and I have, which God has made. This is the freedom that to God is so valuable that he would send his son into the world, and that he would allow his son to die rather than to violate that freedom. God made us and created in us this extraordinary capacity to say "Yes" and to say "No." To say "Yes" even to God himself, is an extraordinary thing, but there it is. God made us that way, so we could say “No” to him, but saying “No” to him is the most tragic thing that we can possibly do. The purpose of this gift of freedom with which God made us is so that we can say “Yes” to him. God made us free so that we could truly participate in a relationship with him. It is an extraordinary thing. God made us with this extraordinary capacity to acknowledge, to reciprocate, and to be in relationship with him.

This freedom is at the core of the temptations that Satan entices Jesus with at the beginning of his public life. Satan tells Jesus not to consult human freedom. Don’t reach out to human freedom. Manipulate. Coerce. Bamboozle. Push. Cajole. Do everything you can, but don’t go to human freedom. Don’t make yourself dependent upon human freedom. So Satan says. Yet it was this very thing which Jesus came to do. He came to make himself truly dependent on human freedom at whatever cost. Here in our Church, we contemplate always the cost that Jesus paid so that his mission to the world could truly be an invitation. Jesus’ invitation entirely validates and confirms that extraordinary gift with which we are created, which is the gift of our freedom.

My friends, we too in this world have little regard for that extraordinary gift with which God has made us. When we look at one another, we immediately give in to these temptations. We immediately seek to cajole, to coerce, to get our way without the reverence for the freedom of the other.

We seek to bypass that freedom whenever humanly possible. We seek to escape the drama of the freedom of the other. This is not what God will do. God will not violate that extraordinary gift of our freedom. Instead, he invites us, again and again, to come to him. He gives us once again, as he gave us at our creation, that extraordinary opportunity to say, "Yes, Lord." Mary began this history thirty years before the scene in the desert when meeting the angel. In the fullness of her freedom, Mary— first of a new race, of a new people, of a new lincage—began this history by saying "Yes" to this message that the angel brought to her. She frecly adhered to the plan of God.

God sends his angels to us also. In so many ways, and in so many circumstances of our life, God invites us to be his. To be with him and to begin with him. To live life in him. He invites us to acknowledge and recognize him as the very center of who we are and what we do. My friends, we can comprehend that there is only one possible answer. This is why Jesus shared our condition in everything but sin, because sin isn't an answer at all. Sin is simply giving up of the greatest gift that has been given to us.

As we engage in this Lenten journey then, let's ask that this drama, this great possibility that passes through all of our lives, might emerge to us in more clarity. Let us pray that the invitation of Christ and the great possibility of our "Yes" to Christ may emerge for us as something beautiful, compelling, and attractive. Let us recognize that our "Yes" is *the* way for us, *the* possibility of life for us.

Today's Gospel ends with Satan departing from Jesus for a time. Satan will come back. He'll come back on Good Friday when he thinks this is the time when he can win his definitive victory. We'll meditate on that when the day comes. In the meantime, let us ask that we may never underestimate ourselves. The world today tries to communicate to us in every way it can that we don't really matter that much. Is that not true? Doesn't the world, in one way or another, try to tell us that precisely that freedom, with which God endowed us, doesn't really matter that much and that we should get over it? But the Church will always hold this extraordinary freedom as the most precious gift, and the most inviolable thing with which God has constituted us.

People may have been surprised, indeed they were surprised, by how energetically the Church reacted to one tiny little bit of the Affordable Care Act.[4] The proposed law stepped just a little bit on that gift of freedom with which God made us, and the Church immediately said, no, you can't do this. You can do all the other things, fine. But this you cannot do. You cannot step on my freedom. You cannot get around our freedom. You cannot find some little trick that will resolve the issue because freedom is myself. Freedom is my "I. Freedom is me. Freedom is the most precious thing. My friends, this does matter. This truly does matter. This truly counts. We should never try to get around the freedom of another.

---

[4] The comprehensive health care reform law enacted in March 2010 (referred to as ACA, the Patient Protection Affordable Care Act, or "Obamacare").

When I was in the seminary, there was a man in a different seminary that I used to meet up with. He ended up leaving the seminary after seven years. After leaving he told me, "You know, every time I had a doubt about my vocation and I went to talk to one of my superiors, they'd always give me some new responsibility, or they'd promote me, or they'd give me something that would make me get over it." And when I heard that, I said, "What a terrible thing to do to a human being. Instead of saying 'yes, look, pay attention, consider, discern, judge, decide, and conclude what it is you truly want' there was this stubborn attempt to make the person go forward with less than the fullness of their freedom." We need never to do that, my friends. We should not try to get our friends to do the things that we want them to do with anything less than the fullness of their freedom. Because when we do that, we truly betray them.

Let us ask that we may have an extraordinary reverence for ourselves above all. Unless we have it for ourselves, we will never have it for anyone else. Let us ask that we might have a reverence for this extraordinary freedom for which Jesus turned down these three apparent shortcuts that Satan offered him to accomplish his mission without suffering. Let us treasure this extraordinary gift of freedom for which Jesus ultimately died on the cross. We can choose not the manipulations but rather to run the gauntlet to the end of that extraordinary creation which is freedom. Let us ask for growth in our culture to honor the freedom of one another in a world that always seeks to diminish us more and more. Let us ask that we may defeat the temptation to live lives that are small in our relationships with our family and in our community.

February 18, 2018
First Sunday of Lent

READINGS

First Reading: Genesis 9:8-15
Second Reading: 1 Peter 3:18-22
Gospel Reading: Mark 1:12-15

COLLECT

Grant, almighty God, through the yearly observances of holy Lent, that we may grow in understanding of the riches hidden in Christ and by worthy conduct pursue their effects. Through our Lord Jesus Christ, your Son, who lives and reigns with you in the unity of the Holy Spirit, one God, for ever and ever.

Covenant

Today's readings are all centered on a very vital dimension of the relationship between God and man, which is a relationship of covenant. What is covenant? Well, a covenant is a relationship that is established by an agreement between two parties. This is the supreme model in our ordinary life, and especially in the marriage model. A marriage is a covenant; it is an agreement. It is two parties who set their minds, their hearts, and their souls on one great and true goal. The relationship with God is the goal precisely because God created man in freedom, and a relationship expresses that. God doesn't want to violate that freedom but yet wants to bring us back to communion with him. He wants to bring us back to communion with him without using coercion, force, or some magical trick. It's for this reason that God entered our world. Jesus wants to reconcile us to our heavenly Father, as one of the Collects of this Lenten season says, "Again, and again you offered a covenant to man."

In the first reading we hear about the second great covenant that God offers to man. The first covenant was offered to Adam and Eve. The second covenant, this covenant, is offered with Noah. Noah has come out of the ark, with all those who were with him, and all those animals of the world. And the Lord offers them a covenant of his benevolence toward all his creatures. In this reading of Genesis, at the dawn of Israel, a chosen people, we see that God wants to reach everyone. This covenant that God makes with Noah is a covenant with all of the created order, everything that God has made. Remember that the flood has just destroyed all things. And now God makes all things anew with this covenant, which is signed with the appearance of the rainbow in the sky. That is a promise of God, to which God is always faithful. Just because God offers a new covenant, it doesn't mean that the old covenant passes away. None of God's covenants pass away. So, this beautiful and simple covenant that God made at the beginning of our history with Noah is a covenant that he still honors. When we look at that rainbow in the sky we can constantly be reminded of the covenant of benevolence toward all that is in the world. This is a beautiful thing, but this is only the first of several covenants.

During the Sundays of Lent, in the first reading, we will continue to read the history of salvation. If you attend the Easter vigil you will know that at the beginning we read seven readings from the Old Testament that lead us through all of the salvation history up to the coming of Christ. We do this for everyone during the season of Lent because we need readings that show us the history of salvation. And we begin here with Noah and with God's promise that he will not wipe out the world again.

There are two parties in a covenant. One of the parties in this covenant is humanity, and through Noah all of humanity. The problem here is that humanity does not honor or obey the covenant. Humanity continually betrays the covenants that God makes with man. However many times man fails, God draws man again and again into a new covenant. This is the point of the covenant with Noah; God will not continue to wipe out humanity because we are unfaithful to his covenants. Instead, God continually proposes a new covenant. We will see in the coming weeks how God creates covenant after covenant: in the first covenant, in Noah; the second covenant, in Abraham; the third covenant, in Moses; the fourth covenant, in David.

The fifth and final covenant fulfills the preceding covenants. It is the covenant described by Saint Peter in the second reading. He describes the relationship that God has established with man in the final covenant. The fifth covenant in Jesus Christ is a very, very special covenant because God sends his son. When God made the covenant with humanity with Noah, who spoke for humanity? It was Noah. When God made the covenant with humanity in Abraham, who spoke for humanity? It was Abraham. There was always a person. Noah, Abraham, Moses, David. There was always a person. So, what does Christ do? God himself enters history and becomes a man so that Christ can now be the one who stands and makes a promise to God. Christ makes peace between humanity and God. This extraordinary peace comes from this covenant under which we live.

This covenant is extraordinary because in previous covenants, the ratification of the covenant was humanity's fidelity to our part of the covenant. And it had to be accomplished by all of humanity. Who is it that breaks the covenants again and again? It's not Noah, Abraham, Moses, or David. It's humanity. What happens in this final covenant? This is what changes very profoundly and deeply the Christian way of life from before the sacrifice of Christ on the cross. When Christ gave his own body—true God, and true man—he paid the price for us. He was one of us and he pays the full price of this covenant in his sacrifice on Calvary. The difference is this covenant is not entrusted to our coherence, our morality, our being able to be good. It is won, it is already ratified, fulfilled, and made complete by Christ's sacrifice on the cross.

What does that mean for us? It means that living this covenant is living a relationship with Christ. To live in the new covenant is not to renew our efforts to be good (though we should always renew our efforts to be good; that's another issue). What we need to do is follow the main line of the fulfillment of God's holy will through this covenant; and that is how we belong to Christ, that we live and dwell in him. In this way we are with Christ and the covenant is fulfilled for us with Christ.

Walking with Christ makes me think of someone going into an important institution where, because of security checks, you can't just walk in unless you are with one of the bosses of that institution. And you know, the boss goes through security, and then the guard looks at you with a question mark and you say, "Oh, I'm with him." That is the way we get in. We need Jesus to say, when we come to judgment, "He's with me." That's the way that Jesus wants to save us, by us being with him, belonging to him, and having our life in him. This is the way his covenant works. This is also the way of the Christian life; the profound, deep, and continual belonging to

God. And that's what Jesus is offering to us. Jesus is giving us the gift of this belonging to God. Life in Christ.

There's a wonderful book of modern theology called *Living in Christ* by Cardinal Caffarra[5]. (There are many, many books of modern theology, some so thick that you would need a stool to be able to be able to read them all!) This one little book by Cardinal Caffarra describes the Christian moral life and traces out something that can help us to overcome what is sometimes called *moralism.* Moralism is the belief that we are justified by our own morality and that our moral efforts are what save us. If that were the case and we were able to do it ourselves, Christ would not have come. Christ came precisely because we could not do it ourselves. So, in this book Cardinal Caffarra shows how life in Christ leads to the fulfillment of everything that is true, right, and good. From that belonging to Christ there is produced in us the character of the saint. The saint is the one who fulfills the human condition perfectly. Instead of the center of our life being our moral effort, it is our relationship with Christ that can draw us into a perfect fulfillment of everything that the moral law proposes to us. *Through him, with him, and in him*, as we say in Mass.

So, this is the sense of the reading on this first Sunday of Lent: an indication is given to us once again that the heart of this season of Lent is our covenant. Jesus came to Galilee proclaiming the Gospel of God. This is the time of

[5] Carlo Caffara, *Living in Christ: Fundamental Principles of Catholic Moral Teaching* (San Francisco, CA: Ignatius Press, 1987).

fulfillment. The kingdom of God is at hand! Repent and believe in the good news. The good news is precisely the announcement that Christ is coming, that he's with us, and that he invites us to come and follow him. Through that invitation he offers us the fullness of salvation and the accomplishment of everything, even the fulfillment of the law, without one iota passing away.

As we continue this journey in Lent, let us ask that we may focus especially on our relationship with Christ. Let's ask that we might grow in our relationship with Christ. As we heard in the prayer before the reading, if we enter into Christ, we may discover the fullness of the riches that he has to offer us.

February 21, 2016
Second Sunday of Lent

READINGS

First Reading: Genesis 15: 5-12
Second Reading: Philippians 3:17-4:1
Gospel Reading: Luke 9:28B-36

COLLECT

O God, who have commanded us to listen to your beloved Son, be pleased, we pray, to nourish us inwardly by your word, that, with spiritual sight made pure, we may rejoice to behold your glory. Through our Lord Jesus Christ, your Son, who lives and reigns with you in the unity of the Holy Spirit, one God, for ever and ever

The Heavenly Father's Plea

I will try very hard not to put you to sleep with my homily! We hear in this Gospel that the three apostles do fall asleep; not during a prolonged homily but at one of the greatest and most important moments in Jesus' life. One of the things that hints at the fact that there is something very important happening here is repetition. Try to think about another moment in which these very same three fell asleep. It was another very important moment in the life of Jesus. Perhaps you know it already; it is the moment of Jesus' passion in the garden of Gethsemane. When Jesus was suffering his agony, these very same three disciples fall asleep.

What is the connection between these two extraordinary moments? It has sometimes been commented that there is a deep connection between the transfiguration and the resurrection. Perhaps the readings here are pointing us to a deeper and more profound connection between this moment and the passion and death of Jesus. In fact, I think it is true to say that the transfiguration of Jesus could be understood as the Father's gift of Christ to the world. Jesus was born in a stable at Bethlehem, Jesus grew to the adult state, and Jesus lived his public ministry, all of this in obedience to his Father. Now, as we are about to enter the period in which the world rejects Jesus, really rejects him, it is like the Father says, "Watch. Obey him. Listen to him. Follow him." The Father commends Jesus to us, even as the Father, in some sense, acknowledges and offers us the entire redemptive work of Christ.

We see that offering before the voice from heaven is heard. We see that Jesus is standing there, revealed in his glory, and talking with these two great prophets of the Old Testament. In the Gospels, only Luke tells us this. Jesus is talking about the exodus that he is about to accomplish in Jerusalem. What is this exodus? It is the departure and the rescue of the people of Israel from slavery in Egypt, and Moses is leading them out of that slavery. The exodus that Jesus is about to accomplish is the leading of us out of the bond of sin into an entirely new life, which is life in him. He is leading us to a new Promised Land, to a new reality. We are going with Jesus to a new human reality in which we share in his life. That exodus will come through the cross of Christ. Every time Jesus mentioned the cross, his apostles were horrified. They couldn't possibly imagine that the great adventure through which they had been following Jesus these last years could have that ending. It is for this reason that Jesus offers them a moment to see his glory revealed.

Luke's Gospel goes a little bit deeper and reveals precisely that the Father offers us Jesus. In the Father's love, he sends his only son. So, the death of Jesus on the cross is not just a sacrifice of Jesus; it is a sacrifice of the Father in heaven also. The Father gives us his son and says to do with him as you will. I give him to you. I give him to your freedom. I entrust him to you. Jesus knows how the world will deal with this.

He understands what the response will be when his Father offers him to the world. Jesus accepts and embraces that exodus which he goes to perform in Jerusalem.

Yet the disciples keep falling asleep. First the three apostles fall asleep here on this mountain. Then they fall asleep as Jesus contemplates his passion and death in the garden of Gethsemane. The letter to the Philippians, with which we opened the Mass, begins with this rejection: "For many, as I have often told you, and now tell you, even in tears, conduct themselves as enemies of the cross of Christ." Enemies of the cross of Christ. Who are these enemies of the cross of Christ? These enemies are us, my friends. They are not some strange people far away who oppose the cross of Christ, they were the apostles that couldn't contemplate this reality. They are also us, who are so reticent to truly be with Jesus. We who are unwilling to bet everything on Jesus and to obey the Father, who says, "This is my beloved son, listen to him." (Luke 9:35) We are unwilling to adhere to him and to face everything with him, and in him.

My friends, this Lenten season is given to us precisely for this opportunity to enter into a deeper awareness of who we are and what it is we want. We are given this time to discover more truly the response that Jesus is to the deepest yearnings of our heart. Rather than mediate with Jesus on the basis of our own conceived outcomes, we need to simply experience what he will do in our lives. If things go well, then Jesus is great. If things go badly, then Jesus is not so great. We look for other points of support. We look for other strategies for living life. This is who the enemies of the cross are. The enemies of the cross aren't to be found in some idea, but they're to be found in an experience in which we tend to hedge our bets. Especially when things are difficult, circumstances are hard, and life is challenging, we look for a strategy that doesn't rely on Jesus' saving grace.

This is precisely when the heavenly Father pleads with us. It is like this moment in the Gospel when he begs us to listen to his son. "Listen to my son." However, the world will not listen to his son. The world will proceed with its own plans, and therefore Jesus will accomplish the great Passover. Jesus will accomplish the great exodus for us by his death and his resurrection. In this way, Jesus will lead us out. It is for this reason that the cross is the way our freedom is accomplished. It is for this reason that Jesus is the way we overcome that resistance. The way we wake up instead of falling asleep is through Jesus himself and his victory. Jesus does not ask us to do something extraordinary, he simply invites us to share his life. He invites us to be with him. To walk daily with him is to have a daily awareness of his presence and to listen to him. Jesus isn't looking for heroes. He is the almighty divine hero that wins for us the great victory. All he invites us to do is use our freedom to consent to a journey with him.

In both Gospel accounts where the apostles fall asleep, Jesus wakes them up and brings them with him. And they accompany him. So, my friends, one of the most consoling things that Jesus reveals to us in this is that it's not up to us to save the world or even ourselves. Jesus has already accomplished that. Jesus has already accomplished the salvation of the world. Jesus has already accomplished our salvation. Now he taps us on the shoulders, and he says, let's go.

Let us ask that throughout this Lenten season, we may be ready to get up when Jesus taps us on the shoulders and wakes us from our slumber. Let us ask that we may be willing to go with him and do the simple thing of remaining with Jesus. Then we'll see the greatness of the victory that he accomplishes. Then we will experience the exodus and the freedom of our lives from the tyranny of everything that is less than our God.

As we celebrate this Mass, we ask for this grace, that through our Lenten observance we may be awakened to stay with Christ and to journey with Christ through the celebrations of Holy Week to the victory of Easter.

March 13, 2016
Fifth Sunday of Lent – Year A. The Third Scrutiny[6]

READINGS

First Reading: Ezekiel 37:12-14
Second Reading: Romans 8:8-11
Gospel Reading: John 11:1-45

COLLECT

By your help, we beseech you, Lord our God, may we walk eagerly in that same charity with which, out of love for the world, you Son handed himself over to death. Through our Lord Jesus Christ, your Son, who lives and reigns with you in the unity of the Holy Spirit, one God, for ever and ever.

---

[6] Rite of Christian Initiation of Adults (RCIA).

Room to Maneuver

We often like to keep things as remote from ourselves as possible. When we hear things said in general, we are very slow to apply them to ourselves. This is a little bit the game that the Pharisees and the Sanhedrin, the leadership of Israel, were playing in today's Gospel. As long as Jesus was out there in the sticks in Galilee it was OK, people could get excited up there, but they need not really have to worry about it. They did not have to give any answer to the question that the life and presence of Jesus was posing to the people who were encountering him. So, they kept that distance. These leaders enjoyed the benefit of distance that kept them from having to give any hard answer to the *Jesus question* that was on everybody's lips.

It seems very clear in Saint John's Gospel that Jesus's decision to go to the suburbs of Jerusalem to raise Lazarus from the dead was a definite turn in the life of Jesus toward the fulfillment of his great salvific work. He knew in turning toward Jerusalem that he was turning also toward the ultimate sacrifice of his life for our salvation. Indeed, his disciples even knew this, because when Jesus decided to go, they said they wanted to go too and die with him. They knew that when Jesus went to Jerusalem he was bringing the fight to the core of the people of Israel. He was taking away that room for maneuver that the leadership of Israel were keeping for themselves by keeping Jesus at a distance.

There are many hints that Lazarus came from a well-to-do family. One indicator is seen in the people who had come out to console the family – the Jews. When John says that many of the Jews had come to console Martha and Mary, he doesn't just mean any of the people of Israel, but he means the leadership of Israel. When Jesus works this extraordinary and beautiful miracle for his friend, he does so right there in front of these leaders of Israel. In this way Jesus brings the question right to the feet of the Sanhedrin itself. And in some way he is also bringing about those circumstances that will lead immediately to his passion and his death.

On passion Sunday, we will read the passion Gospel where Jesus turns definitively toward that event. He chooses that. Many of the things that Jesus says in today's Gospel refer not just to the things that he is going to do for Lazarus, but to the great thing that he is going to do for love of all of us.

This strategy of trying to escape a decision is an eternal strategy of ours. We take a step away from what is said, or we don't engage with what is going on. Today I would like to take a moment to talk about this because in the parish we are trying to promote the work of our Saint Vincent de Paul society, which is a very important dimension of our parish life. I know that we are all called to practice charity in every moment and perhaps right now just moving over and making a little bit more room for the person in the pew beside you, you're practicing the virtue of charity. However, the Society of Saint Vincent de Paul is our particular work of helping those in need in our community. It also is a powerful instrument for the visibility of Christ.

I would like to take just a moment to tell you about how this organization started. Frederic Ozanam was a gentleman, as they used to call them in those days. He was a man from the upper part of society. He was a student and then eventually a teacher at the Sorbonne University in Paris, which was the most prestigious university in Paris at the time and is still a great and prestigious university. There he was in a very secular and anti-Christian environment. Already that environment was strong and flourishing during his time there. Frederic Ozanam had put together a debating society where he welcomed all challenges. He would say to the university community that if anyone has anything that they would like to say to us that you think would shut us down, you come and tell us, and we'll listen. We'll take into account what you say. Come. Open and fair debate. Many people did come, and they had many debates. Frederic Ozanam was a student of Maurice Blondel and of the great Catholic tradition that brought us so many great thinkers of the faith of that time. He won his debates pretty handsomely for the most part, people would report.

At a certain point he realized that winning those debates wasn't winning any converts to Christ. It is not as though atheists who had come to debate him would leave saying, "Oh, yeah, well I guess Professor Ozanam won that debate today so I'd better become a Christian." None did. Neither his audience nor his debaters were drawn to the faith by the marvels of his intellect and his ability to defend the faith. Frederic Ozanam started to think a lot about this. He eventually thought about something that Pope Francis has said to us – that faith comes through an encounter with Christ. So he recognized that winning a debate was not causing anyone to have an encounter with Christ.

It was from this thought that the Society of Saint Vincent de Paul was born. It was born as an effort to practice gratuitous love and charity. Frederic Ozanam's society is not a project for social reform, but a project of love, a turning toward love. Frederic came to understand that in expressing the love of Christ through acts of charity he would be making Christ visible in the world. Frederic realized that through charitable work he could more effectively do what he was trying to do, which was to offer a contrast to the mentality of his age. (The mentality of his age was like an early version of the mentality of our own age.) And indeed, the Society of Saint Vincent de Paul grew like wildfire. Once it was established, it spread to parishes throughout France, then beyond France, and then eventually to our shores, where there are thousands of chapters in parishes throughout our land. Many people were converted to Christ through the work of the Saint Vincent de Paul society.

Six months ago we gave birth to a Saint Vincent de Paul conference here at Nativity. That word *conference* gives a little hint to its origin in the debates that Frederic Ozanam used to have, because debates were called conferences. The society he formed was like the ultimate conference. The ultimate conference wasn't full of wise and great arguments for the faith, but it was a life of charity, practiced by him and his friends and the many other friends that would join him.

Those friends have now been joined by our Saint Vincent de Paul society right here at Nativity. Already we see the same dynamic where people don't just get some help, but people are attracted by and come to know Christ. People come back to Church and people who have never been to Church start coming.

This is not totally disjointed from the Gospel we were talking about before because this is also the way that Jesus works in the world today. In the world, Jesus works through the Church, doing the very same thing that he did by going to the house of Lazarus and raising him from the dead. Jesus brings the proposal to us and provokes us with questions. What are those people doing? Why do they do that? What is this all about? Jesus invites us to join in that discussion.

We now have this Saint Vincent de Paul society, a great gift of our parish—and it's ours. From its very beginning, the Saint Vincent de Paul society was parish based. Frederic Ozanam started the first society in his own parish and now Nativity has its own Saint Vincent de Paul conference. I would like you to consider what God might be calling you to do and not to put the decision on the back burner. Let's not say, "He's talking about the guy on my left and on my right, but he's not really talking about me right now." That's what the Pharisees in Jerusalem were doing. We don't want to do that because the work of Christ involves us.

What would we like to do? Would we like to join and be the hands, feet, mouth, and brains that work on behalf of our brothers and sisters in need? Would we like to be members of the Saint Vincent de Paul conference giving our time and our talent? Would we like to contribute financially? As you know, today everything gets reduced to money—I mean everything passes through that medium. Our conference is always in need of the ability to actually address the concrete needs of the people and so be able to express love for each person. Whether it be assistance with rent, a utility bill that can't be paid, the need to fill a prescription at the drug store, or whatever form that assistance might take, if there's no money in the bank, we have to say, "We love you, bye-bye." It's not that convincing.

I'd like you to consider those two things: being a member and how to contribute. The third issue applies to everyone, which is to pray for the Saint Vincent de Paul members. I know that sometimes for them it can be a dramatic way of living because every day they are seeing the needs that people fall into, and the inability of society, even with the government's billions, to answer the needs of all of the people. The members must also hold on to the awareness that our Saint Vincent de Paul conference won't fix the world. But then again, from its very origin, it was never about fixing the world. It was about offering to the world the visibility of Christ, who alone can truly fix the world and fix the human heart.

March 24, 2016
Holy Thursday – The Mass of the Lord's Supper

READINGS

First Reading: Exodus 12:1-8, 11-14
Second Reading: 1 Corinthians 11:23-26
Gospel Reading: John 13:1-15

COLLECT

O God, who have called us to participate in this most sacred Supper, in which your Only Begotten Son, when about to hand himself over to death, entrusted to the Church a sacrifice new for all eternity, the banquet of his love, grant, we pray, that we may draw from so great a mystery, the fullness of charity and of life. Through our Lord Jesus Christ, your Son, who lives and reigns with you in the unity of the Holy Spirit, one God, for ever and ever.

The Fullness of Life

The last lines of the Gospel we just read are the very opening lines of the great farewell discourse of Jesus. The last lines are ones in which he in some way recapitulates the whole of his mission and the whole of his journey. These lines are also, in some way, how he explains what it is he came into the world to do. He confronts, again in those moments, the opposition and the impermeability of the human heart that he found when he came into the world. That very discourse lasts through three entire chapters of John's Gospel and then concludes in a fourth chapter which is the priestly prayer of Jesus, a prayer in which he stands as priest before the Father asking for and bringing about the salvation of the world. If we were to try to synthesize, in one single expression from that prayer of his, the very core of his mission, we couldn't do better than to fix on that phrase in which he said that *he came so that we might have life*. His mission for the world was the gift of life to us.

This word *life* that Jesus uses is not just the period during which the organism of the human being is alive, but it is a fullness of life which we hardly even begin to suspect is possible. This is the life which he came to give to us and to offer us. Jesus himself tells us what that life is and perhaps the answer he gives is surprising to us. He says, "And life, eternal life, that life that I come to give you is this: that you might know the Father, and the one that he has sent, Jesus Christ." (John 17:3) This is the fullness of that life. This is the origin and the root of the experience of that word *life* that transcends and blows right open our concept of living. This fullness of life is a possibility that so exceeds what we expect and come to think of as following day after day. The fullness of life is to know the Father, and who he has sent, Jesus Christ. This is the fullness of life. It is for this that Jesus has done everything that he has done. It is for this reason that he gets up from the table and washes his disciples' feet. Washing the disciple's feet is not just one more little sign that Jesus throws in for good measure at the Last Supper. Everything in John's Gospel tells us that this gesture is entirely connected to the following four chapters, which are placed within the context of that Last Supper, and therefore, express for us the fullness of the mystery of the revelation of our redemption.

This gesture of the washing of the feet is part of that farewell discourse. It is part of that priestly prayer. As Jesus' bequest to his beloved, it is full of meaning. Although we can only begin to scratch the surface of its meaning, Jesus wants us to know that we must love one another as he has loved us. And therefore, he introduces us to a completely new way of life. Jesus here does not say that you must love one another as you love yourselves; he says you must love one another as I, Jesus, have loved you. And my friends, nothing is greater, more beautiful, and more extraordinary in our Christian vocation than to know the immensity of that life to which we are called. Nothing is greater than the extraordinary nature of that life to which we are called. We are called to love one another *as Jesus loved us*. As Jesus is loving us in these very deeds that he carries out, in this washing of the feet and in all that will flow out from that moment in the days that follow.

It is for this that we have life; to know the one true God and the one whom he has sent. It is for this life that he instituted the Eucharist foreshadowed so powerfully in the Passover of the people of Israel in Egypt. Already the Eucharist was received and was being lived in the life of the nascent Church by Saint Paul as described in his letter to the Corinthians. On this altar 2,000 years later, it is still being celebrated by us tonight. Here is the Eucharist in an unbroken chain from that Last Supper to this evening, passing through every circumstance the world could have possibly imagined. The Eucharist continues through persecutions and every kind of adverse circumstance. I think for a moment of those hidden priests in Elizabethan times, around 1558, who went throughout England celebrating the Mass in closets, hiding away and escaping through priest holes. Through all these circumstances, through 2,000 years, this Eucharist has lived and been the instrument by which Christ continues to communicate that gift of life to the Church.

It is for this life that Jesus instituted the other great sacrament that we celebrate tonight, the sacrament of Holy Orders; the ordained priesthood. This is not a priesthood of its own, or a priesthood of some powers given to a human being, but a very participation in the priesthood of Christ himself. In Christianity, ultimately there is one priest, and that priest is Christ. Through the sacrament that Jesus institutes this night, he entrusts to his ordained ministers, the gift of being able to act truly in his name. As the tradition of the Church says, a priest is *In Persona Christi*, as Christ. You'll notice both in the sacrament of Confession and in the blessed Eucharist that at the moment the priest comes to the celebration of those sacraments, he no longer uses a third person, he's no longer talking about Christ, but he uses the first person, because in that moment he is *In Persona Christi*. He is in the person of Christ. And that, my friends, is the great sacrament whose institution we celebrate tonight together with the celebration of the institution of the Eucharist. That sacrament of Holy Orders, by which living in the world is this voice, this authority of Christ that can say "I absolve you from your sins." In this expression it is Christ that speaks through the sacramental ministry of the priest, not the priest himself. Christ is the one who is doing the forgiving. Christ is the one who acts.

These are the gifts that Christ gives to the Church, and he gives them so we might have that life where we know the one true God and the one he has sent, Jesus Christ. My friends, it is in knowing him that all things become clear. It is only in knowing Jesus that man stands up, that man becomes self, that man becomes alive. It is only in knowing him that man becomes glorious and gives glory to God. Anything less than this life and man is disappointing to himself and to God who made him for the fullness of life. Clearly to say that God is disappointed is anthropomorphic language, but it does express a reality of what God has wanted and desired: the heart of man. When man withholds his heart from God, God has chosen to suffer that withholding. So, my friends, the celebration of the Last Supper brings us to the very core of the mystery of Christ's mission, of Christ himself, of our encounter with God and Christ.

As we continue our journey now, in the celebration of the great events of our salvation in these coming days, let us ask that we might be moved. Let us pray that something might happen in us that we are incapable of producing in ourselves, but to which we must open the door and for which we must beg, which is that we might know the One True God and the one he has sent. Anything less than this, my friends, is truly intolerable. Let us ask the Lord for the gift of this grace.

March 26, 2016
Holy Saturday
At the Easter Vigil in the Holy Night of Easter

READINGS

First Reading: Genesis 1:1-2:2
Second Reading: Genesis 22:1-18
Reading 3: Exodus 14:15-15:1
Reading 4: Isaiah 54:5-14
Reading 5: Isaiah 55:1-11
Reading 6: Baruch 3:9-15, 32-4:4
Reading 7: Ezekiel 36:16-17A, 18-28
Epistle: Romans 6:3-11
Gospel Reading: Luke 24:1-12

COLLECT

O God, who make this most sacred night radiant with the glory of the Lord's Resurrection, stir up in your Church a spirit of adoption, so that, renewed in body and mind, we may render you undivided service. Through our Lord Jesus Christ, your Son, who lives and reigns with you in the unity of the Holy Spirit, one God, for ever and ever.

The Risen Christ Found

The very first announcement of Jesus's resurrection was a question. Why are you looking for the living among the dead? Why are you looking for the one who is alive among the dead? This great question is answered for us once again tonight. Jesus is alive. That's the great resounding proclamation of tonight. Jesus is alive, active, and in the world. Jesus is present. He touches our lives today as he touched the lives of people 2,000 years ago.

On this Easter night, we have the extraordinary grace to receive eleven people into the Church. These people will begin the journey of their Christian faith through baptism. By encountering our community of faith, they have become persuaded that Jesus is alive. They found the evidence among us that Jesus is alive in the world. They encountered that evidence in an experience of life that drew their attention and made this question about whether Jesus is alive or not compelling for them. As they drew closer, as they studied, worked, and prayed; and as they engaged in charity, they came to perceive ever more clearly and certainly, experience by experience, that indeed Jesus is alive. So firm is their belief that momentarily they will come before the altar and be led to the baptismal font where they will receive new life from him.

My friends, this is an instance of Jesus alive. This event that is taking place in our community, one of extraordinary proportions, is the baptism of our brothers and sisters. No longer infants, these candidates have made this journey through their own convictions. Based on the evidence that they themselves have been able to perceive, they have come to affirm their faith. Illuminated by the grace of Christ, they have come to say, moments before their baptism, "I do. I do. I do." This is 2,000 years that have passed, my friends, and believers are still gathered around his altar. This community of the baptized to which Christ gives life continues to persevere in a world in which we always have to struggle. We all know very well the particular and dramatic struggles of our time and the struggles of our faith in our time. But we hold on tenaciously, because we have come to know that Jesus is alive. My friends, that's the beauty of this night.

The beautiful vigil readings and the beautiful psalms we chant between each reading are the content of this night. The glorious chanting of the Gloria and the Alleluia which just preceded the reading of this Gospel announce to those women who in the very normality of the grief for a beloved deceased, go to the tomb. These women are not expecting anything more than what normally happens at the tombs; that they will go there in silence and say their prayers. Maybe they plan to leave some votive, or sentimental gift, and eventually withdraw. Instead they meet two angels who proclaim, "Why are you looking for one who is alive among the dead?" (Luke 24:5) My friends, Jesus is alive. Let us rejoice and be glad.

March 27, 2016
The Resurrection of the Lord
The Mass of Easter Day

READINGS

First Reading: Acts of the Apostles 10:34A, 37-43
Second Reading: 1 Corinthians 5:6B-8
Sequence - Victimae paschali laudes
Gospel Reading: John 20:1-9

COLLECT

O God, who on this day, through your Only Begotten Son, have conquered death and unlocked for us the path to eternity, grant, we pray, that we who keep the solemnity of the Lord's Resurrection may, through the renewal brought by your Spirit, rise up in the light of life. Through our Lord Jesus Christ, your Son, who lives and reigns with you in the unity of the Holy Spirit, one God, for ever and ever.

Turn Your Gaze

One of the consequences of Christianity coming to the Roman Empire was that the very concept of time changed. Historians tell us that for the Romans, time was a cyclical thing. Every year was basically and fundamentally the same as the year preceding it. The year just repeated, and repeated, and repeated. Again and again the same cycle. A human being got to be in the world for a certain number of those cycles and that was it. When Christianity came to the world, the historians noticed a change in the way that time is thought about. Time is conceived of in a linear fashion. Instead of every year just being a repeat of the previous year, the years are now a journey through time toward destiny. Each year is another step on that great journey toward the fulfillment and fullness of life.

Engineers, scientists, and sociologists use the phrase *changing the equation.* We have heard it used concerning some of the wars we've had. The media tells us that we need to do something that changes the equation. By that phrase they are describing a desire to get out of a situation where you just keep doing the same thing and the same thing keeps happening. Maybe you change a few little things in the process, but it is not enough to change the cycle and make something completely new happen. For example, maybe you get a five percent raise one day at work. Yes, it's good, it makes things a bit easier, and it gives you a little more fluidity, but it doesn't change the equation. Fundamentally everything is the same. Probably thc house stays the same, the car stays the same, the schools stay the same, and the activities stay the same. Things are a little bit easier, but it's basically the same loop. If you were to win the lottery, now that would change the equation. All of a sudden, everything would have to be thought about in a new way and new possibilities would open up. The following year would be different than the year that preceded it. That's what we mean by *changing the equation.*

My friends, the event that we celebrated at the vigil and on Easter Sunday is *the* event that changes the equation. It's the only event that really and truly changes the equation. It's for that reason that the historical idea of time being a cycle was defeated, and the idea of time being a journey became dominant.

All of us sometimes can feel that we run on a treadmill. We just keep running, and running, and running but nothing ever changes. You know, when you are on the treadmill you keep running and all you see is the stairs, the basement, and maybe a little video screen or something that you have there to entertain you. But when you go outside and run, everything changes, constantly. Every turn is something new. A new vision. We sometimes feel that we are trapped on the treadmill of life and that no matter how hard we run, nothing really changes. Well, breaking this cycle is what this day is about.

This day is about the possibility of a huge and a great change. Jesus Christ, by rising from the dead, brings that change to all of life. In the beautiful sequence that we sang and that was chanted for us here, one of the verses said:

> Tell us, O Mary, what you saw when you went there. Tell us what you saw early in the morning!

The Church longs and waits to hear again and again, and we never tire of hearing each Easter about that great event that truly gives us hope and means that life is opened up. Life is not just the things we do anymore, but now life is a journey of the whole of our humanity into hope. The things in our life, the fixed assets in our life may stay the same. But if we attach ourselves to Christ, if we follow him, if we really pay attention to him, you cannot imagine the things that will happen. If we draw close to Christ and we allow him to become the effective center of our life, an unimaginable change of scenery awaits us just around the next corner. Life becomes beautiful and exciting. Life becomes full of love and goodness. Life is lived with the ability to face trials without being crushed. Life becomes something truly good, as Peter says when Jesus was transfigured on the mountain; "It is good that we are here." (Matthew 17:4)

The Transfiguration was a foreshadowing of the event we celebrate today on Easter where Jesus is revealed in all his glory. Now living in glory, he invites us, continually and always, to a relationship him. This relationship changes the equation big time! It will break us out of that treadmill and allow us to see beautiful things that our heart longs for. This relationship will allow us to receive true comfort. Just think of that word *comfort* for a moment. What is truly comforting? Do we find that the biggest comfort in this world is forgetfulness? How could forgetfulness really be hopeful?

The comfort that Jesus brings is a comfort in the midst of everything. It's not that the trials will disappear, or all our obstacles will be overcome, but that in our hearts there will burn a trust and a confidence so great that we can truly walk on water. We can be like Peter who walked across the raging water to Christ. My friends, this is what we celebrate at Easter. It's a possibility and a reality for every one of us. It is very, very likely that everyone here around this altar in such numbers this morning is baptized. That means his life is already in you. You do not need to do anything. There is no program that you have to go through to bring you close to Christ. All you have to do is invite him and say "Yes" to him. Just turn your gaze to him. I am sure you have heard people say, "I'm a convert." The word convert really means to turn your gaze. The original Latin of *convert* means to turn around and look somewhere else. My friends, that's what Jesus invites us to do, to turn around and look at him. When we fix our gaze on him we can learn what the journey of life is like. Jesus will lead us into many things that we might not have expected, but through them he will bring to our lives the greatness of joy and the peace of a contented heart.

My friends, Jesus died and rose again to introduce us to this experience. He rose again so that he could be with us. Not 2,000 years distant in history, but with us today. Jesus is offering us that gift of life and he makes that offer to us each day. The only thing that can stand in the way of God's giving us the fullness of life is our freedom. Because if we say no, God will wait. He'll wait outside the door and continue to knock from time to time, through circumstances of life. He'll never barge in through that door when we're saying no. He waits, and pleads, and begs for us to say yes to him.

My friends, this Easter, let us hear that pleading voice. Let us say, as Saint John Paul II said on the balcony of Saint Peter's when he came out for the first time as Pope, and I find myself quoting every Easter morning, "Throw open wide the doors of your heart to Christ. Let him enter."[7] Many years later, Pope Benedict XVI came out on that same balcony and said:

> Christ comes to take nothing from you, nothing that can add one iota to your happiness. Christ comes to take nothing but to give all.[8]

---

[7] "Homily of Pope John Paul II for the Inauguration of His Pontificate," Saint Peter's Square, Sunday, October 22, 1978, http://www.vatican.va/content/john-paul-ii/en/homilies/1978/documents/hf_jp-ii_hom_19781022_inizio-pontificato.html.

[8] "Mass, Imposition of the Pallium and Conferral of the Fisherman's Ring for the Beginning of the Petrine Ministry of the Bishop of Rome, Homily of His Holiness Benedict XVI," Saint Peter's Square, Sunday, April 24, 2005, http://www.vatican.va/content/benedict-xvi/en/homilies/2005/documents/hf_ben-xvi_hom_20050424_inizio-pontificato.html.

As we celebrate the resurrection of Jesus from the dead, let us be willing to think big. Let us be willing to imagine, dream, and ask for something truly great. Not just for a slightly better day, not just for a slightly better loop on the treadmill, or on the cycle of life, but something truly great and beautiful that truly sets us free. Christ came for this, and he's willing and waiting to give it to us. Let us ask that each one of us, this year, might embrace it with all our heart and all our soul. God bless you all.

April 03, 2016
Second Sunday of Easter
(or Sunday of Divine Mercy)

READINGS

First Reading: Acts of the Apostles 5:12-16
Second Reading: Revelations 1:9-11A, 12-13, 17-19
Gospel Reading: John 20:19-31

COLLECT

God of everlasting mercy, who in the very recurrence of the paschal feast kindle the faith of the people you have made your own, increase, we pray, the grace you have bestowed, that all may grasp and rightly understand in what font they have been washed, by whose Spirit they have been reborn, by whose Blood they have been redeemed. Through our Lord Jesus Christ, your Son, who lives and reigns with you in the unity of the Holy Spirit, one God, for ever and ever.

God's Enduring Mercy

Thomas was the one who most harshly expressed his skepticism when he heard the news of Jesus' resurrection from the dead. But he wasn't the only who was skeptical at first. In yesterday's Gospel we read again, and again, and again, "But they didn't believe. They didn't believe." (Mark 16:11) This was said about the very same group of apostles who were gathered there in the upper room. After he's shown his hands and feet to Thomas, Jesus nonetheless says to him, "Blessed are those who have not seen and have believed." (John 20:29)

What does it mean to not have seen and to have believed? Well, first of all, Jesus calls this position a *blessed* position. And blessed, at the very core of its meaning, signifies that it is fully human. It is fully human to have believed when you haven't seen. When you haven't seen what? When you have not seen Jesus materially and physically in the flesh. Thomas saw the wounds of Jesus. You and I have not seen the wounds of Jesus in the sense that we have not seen the light that reflects off the flesh of Jesus and enters our eyes. We haven't seen him physically present. Yet we have ample reason for our belief because this very belief is central to our faith. Today we celebrate Divine Mercy Sunday. My friends, we could well say that our belief is God's greatest mercy to us because our belief is the gift of knowledge of him.

Pope Benedict wrote an encyclical letter to the whole Church entitled *God is Love.*[9] This title gets to the very core of the relationship with God to which this Mass belongs. I strongly recommend reading Pope Benedict's letter, but here I simply want to start with the intuition that it is clear from the title itself that love is God's nature. Manifested here before us today is that very love. The greatest sign of God's love for us is his self-revelation, that we know him. The gift of faith is indeed the gift in which life comes to us.

Yesterday and today there have been lines and lines outside the confessional. So much so that we have had to double-up the priests there in confession. And that is a beautiful thing. All of that comes as part of the gift of faith. If you have no faith, you are not at confession. If you have no faith, you won't hear those words, "I absolve you from your sins." So it is with everything in our faith and in our religion. Everything in our Catholic life comes to us through our faith. As if this gift of faith wasn't enough, on this very day, four of our brothers and sisters step forward to the foot of the altar to express precisely the fullness of their Catholic faith. We rejoice in that. "Blessed are they who have not seen and have believed." Blessed are you four who have not seen and who have believed. Blessed are you four who are able to observe, reflect, and comprehend the vast evidence of God's victory over death, and his continuing kingship in the world. Blessed

---

[9] Pope Benedict XVI, "Deus Caritas Est, God Is Love" (Encyclical Letter), Saint Peter's Square, Rome, December 25, 2005, https://d2y1pz2y630308.cloudfront.net/1176/documents/2015/5/Deus%20Caritas%20Est.pdf

are you who are able to step forward today and say, "I believe. I believe, and I accept." In just a few moments you will say that simple phrase in which you announce your acceptance and belief in everything the Catholic Church professes, teaches, and proclaims to be the revelation of God.

Blessed Cardinal John Henry Newman also made this announcement. He was a famous and great convert to Catholicism, founder of the Oxford movement, and one who led so many into Catholic faith. When John Henry Newman had to say that phrase, his reflection was that he didn't know everything that the Catholic Church professes, teaches, and proclaims, but he did know from where it comes. He knew the origin. Therefore Newman knew he could accept everything that the Catholic Church teaches, not because he knew everything, but because he embraced and had faith in God's presence in the world as the energizing force of the Church. He believed in the force of God's presence that allows us to know Christ and to believe in him. He is remembered as saying that if he is walking out of this Church in half an hour and somebody walks up and tells him a belief that he had never heard before and shows him how it's an integral part of the fullness of the Catholic faith, Newman would say he already believes that. Someone asked him, how could he believe it if he didn't know it? His answer was, because of the assent of faith.

So, my beloved four candidates, it is not that you are meant to be experts in theology today, it is that you are meant to do exactly what you are doing, you are meant to trust Christ's living presence here, and his great mercy that endures forever.

What does it mean to say that God's mercy endures forever? It means that it didn't end with the gesture of salvation 2,000 years ago with his resurrection. Nor did it end even with his ascension into heaven, but it continues to accompany us day by day. So, we're going to pass now, without further delay, into the celebration of receiving our four friends into full Communion of the Catholic faith.

April 10, 2016
Third Sunday of Easter

READINGS

First Reading: Acts of the Apostles 5:27, 40B-41
Second Reading: Revelations 5:11-14
Gospel Reading: John 21:1-19

COLLECT

May your people exult forever, O God, in renewed youthfulness of spirit, so that, rejoicing now in the restored glory of our adoption, we may look forward in confident hope to the rejoicing of the day of resurrection. Through our Lord Jesus Christ, your Son, who lives and reigns with you in the unity of the Holy Spirit, one God, for ever and ever.

The Only Question Jesus Has

In this beautiful Gospel reading we find a teaching where we can understand the whole of the journey of the Christian life. We are presented here with the journey of Saint Peter, the apostle. Saint Peter is one of those characters in the Gospel about whose personality we know the most. Across many, many stories, we see the consistency of his personality. What was he like? We know that he was an enthusiastic person, always willing to step forward and to involve his life in that thing that was most compelling to him. Peter always ventured forward; he never held back. But we know also that Peter was a weak man in some ways. We know that sometimes he was dominated by lesser things. Sometimes Peter was weakened by fear as we saw in the case of his betrayal of Jesus. Let us follow the example of Peter for a moment so that we can understand from him something about our own journey to Christ.

The first thing we see in Peter is the weight and awareness of his sin. Peter had betrayed the Lord although he never planned to do so. Peter is not like Judas who set everything up so he could betray the Lord and then carried out his plan. Peter was in the back during Jesus' trial, afraid but trying to be close to the Lord. Even when Peter was in the back, one of the officials of the temple points to him and says, "You too, are from Galilee. You're surely one of his disciples." (Matthew 26:73) And at that moment Peter is seized by fear. At that moment all of his affection and his love for Jesus is suppressed by the fear he feels at the possibility of being dragged into this terrible mock trial that's taking place and where it might lead him. So, Peter betrays Jesus in the instant. We know that just the day before he had said no matter what happens, Jesus, I will go with you. I will die with you. (Matthew 26:35) That is Peter's heart. Peter wants to be one who dies with Christ, but then Peter's poor humanity shrinks in front of the fear.

I often say to the young people I educate, "You know I trust your heart, but I don't trust your will." You and I should be like that with ourselves. We trust our heart. We know what we want. We are all gathered here around the altar, aren't we? We are here this Sunday morning when there are lots of things we could be doing, but we're here. That's a witness of our heart. We really do want to be with Jesus. But then, we also have to acknowledge that when things get tough, or when there are other things complicating our lives, we sometimes fail to live out that heart.

Now what about Peter? The first thing I think you have to notice about Peter in these accounts after Jesus' resurrection, and before his ascent into heaven, before the apostles received the gift of the Holy Spirit, is that Peter is full of a great and deep sorrow. Peter is broken-hearted by his betrayal. He feels true sorrow. The Church calls this *contrition.* The awareness of our sin and the weight of our awareness of our sin is contrition.

My friends, we do not do ourselves any favors when we try to minimize our sin, we really don't. What we end up doing is making ourselves unresponsive to love. We need to allow the sin, our weakness, the failure of our will to accomplish that which we truly desire and want, to be present to us. Yet it is only in this way that we can enter into the drama of God's mercy. Awareness of sin is not the opposite of mercy. Mercy is not saying that sin doesn't matter. Mercy is a creative act of God by which he returns to us everything that we lost in our betrayal. That is very different from saying that it doesn't matter. When we say our sins don't matter, we reduce ourselves and we make of ourselves something poor. Ultimately we make ourselves similar to the animals that live according to instinct and aren't called to anything great. However, we, my friends, are called to something great and therefore our sins do matter. We should never think that in a year of mercy, when we are talking or preaching about mercy, it means sin does not matter. Sin does matter and that is why mercy is so great and beautiful.

Peter is full of this dynamic – we see it again and again in him. In this scene from today's Gospel, we see it particularly where Peter is uneasy. Peter is burdened by that cloud which he perceives he has introduced in his relationship with his beloved Lord. Peter knows he loves his Lord, but he also knows he's betrayed his Lord. We see Peter's love when he jumps out of the boat. As soon as John identifies Jesus, Peter jumps right out of the boat to get to Jesus sooner because he loves his Lord. However, he doesn't know what to say to Jesus or how to heal that wound. We can tell that he does not know what to do because he doesn't stay with Jesus on the shore, as you would expect, after jumping out of the boat to be with him. Peter is the one with his active temperament who goes to the boat and pulls in the net. Probably all the others are around Jesus on the shore. All of this is a witness to the discomfort that Peter is carrying in his soul. He does not know what to do with himself.

Peter is looking for an opportunity. How can I resolve this rupture between me and Jesus? How can I overcome this betrayal? Peter is wondering what to do but he doesn't know how to do it. My friends, we too need to enter in there ourselves. We need to come in front of the Lord in poverty of spirit because we cannot even the accounts with our Lord or make up for our sins. There's one version of the Act of Contrition that says, "And make up for my sins." When people say that I always respond, "No. That's really not a good act of contrition." We are sorry for our sins, we repent of our sins, but we cannot make up for them. That is why mercy is such an extraordinary thing. It does something that we can't do for ourselves. Mercy really is how God recreates what was broken.

I always imagine Peter hanging back a little bit, because he doesn't know how to deal with this situation. Yet he does know that he has to be there. He jumps out of the boat and he's there with the other apostles as they huddle around Jesus. Usually Peter is the first one to speak, but here now he's no longer the first one to speak. He hangs back a bit, mortified, humbled and wondering what will happen. That's when Jesus turns to him with a great and beautiful question. Ultimately this is the only question that Jesus has for you and me. Jesus doesn't ask Peter, "How could you have done such a thing?"

If Jesus had said that to Peter, Peter would have been crushed. Jesus doesn't say, "So that's what you think of me, is it?" Or "What happened to your courage?" Or "Come on, man up a little bit." He doesn't say any of those things. Jesus asks Peter the one question that he can answer. Jesus asks, "Simon, son of John, do you love me?" (John 21:15) My friends, that one question is the question that brings out what is positive in Peter. That question lets the love of Peter for Jesus stand forth as the most vital thing.

I don't know what Peter must have thought when Jesus turned to him and finally said "Simon, son of John, do you love me?" I imagine Peter must have thought, "Phew! OK, finally, here it is. Here it is. Here comes the reckoning. Now Jesus is finally going to deal with me for what I did." Who knows what he imagines Jesus is going to do, but the question is "Do you love me?" Peter suddenly finds that instead of being in an awkward situation, looking at his beloved master and not knowing what to say, he is hearing his master and he is saying, "Yes, Lord." Peter is affirming the one thing in the whole world that he knows is true, I love you. Three times Jesus asks him this question. The third time there is a particular sting for Peter because it reminds him that his betrayal was not once, not twice, but three times. Yet the question that Jesus asks him is for the affirmation of their relationship, which is what is most vital. In the end, Peter's relationship with Jesus is the only thing that matters. "Yes, Lord, you know everything. You know I love you." (John 21:17) What does Jesus do? I always imagine that Peter thought, "Well, as regards being the head guy, you can forget that. I don't know if I'll even get to be an apostle anymore." I imagine Peter thought that he would be demoted, but he probably thought that at least he can still be here with Jesus. However, Jesus doesn't take away anything. He doesn't take away the vocation given to Peter or the very reason why Peter was created and born. Instead of withdrawing the task for which God had made him, Jesus in fact recommissions Peter. Jesus re-affirms the great vocation that Peter received and for which Peter was made.

In the first reading we see Peter actively engaged in fulfilling that vocation as he is answering the Sanhedrin on behalf of the nascent Church under trial. Peter is there answering instead of hiding in the back. This journey of growth that Peter takes up, beginning with the affirmation of his love for Jesus, will ultimately lead Peter to making the ultimate sacrifice. Jesus foretells that Peter will lay down his life for his beloved Lord.

My friends, the journey for us is the same. The awareness and burden of our sin we bring to Jesus, not knowing any solution except his gaze and his mercy. We are not able to resolve the issues of our sins other than by the pure and simple gift of God's creative mercy. God forgives us, and he sends us to fulfill more humbly and more truly the vocation for which each one of us is made. God sends us to our life. He sends us to our fatherhood, to our motherhood, to our spousal relationships, and to all that our baptism implies. He sends us to go and live for him by ultimately giving everything for him. It's unlikely but not impossible that some of us will have to give our lives for Christ as Peter did. We are all called to grow in that relationship as Peter grew and was sent by his Lord. We are all called, and we are all sent –to our own lives and our own vocation. My brothers and sisters, we have to contemplate these things seriously. Our vocations are not secondary aspects of our life; they are our life. Jesus sends us as he says, "Feed my sheep." (John 21:17) In this simple sentence Jesus summarizes the vocation of Peter: feed my sheep. Well my friends, he sends you and me to our vocation too.

Let us ask that in the power of his mercy we may go to live the vocation that God has given us, in its fullness and beauty. Let us live our vocation in its correspondence to everything that our heart wants. Instead of thinking that we are made for something small, let us know that we are made for something great. Jesus will not take away or diminish our vocation, instead he will re-affirm it. Let us ask that we might embrace with our "Yes" that vocation to which he sends us.

May 17, 2015
Solemnity of the Ascension of the Lord

READINGS

First Reading: Acts of the Apostles 1:1-11
Second Reading: Ephesians 4:1-13
Gospel Reading: Mark 16:15-20

COLLECT

Gladden us with holy joys, almighty God, and make us rejoice with devout thanksgiving, for the Ascension of Christ your Son is our exaltation, and, where the Head has gone before in glory, the Body is called to follow in hope. Through our Lord Jesus Christ, your Son, who lives and reigns with you in the unity of the Holy Spirit, one God, for ever and ever.

Advantages of the Ascension

As is so often commented, the moment of Jesus' ascension into heaven seemed immediately to his apostles a terrible loss. They had already lost Jesus when he died on the cross and were completely reborn and rejuvenated when they encountered him alive and risen from the dead. When they found him alive, when he lived with them, ate with them, walked with them, and talked with them again after his resurrection, they were full of joy and peace. Among these teachings after his resurrection, Jesus starts to reference the impending event of his ascension to the right hand of the Father. The Gospels testify to us how terrified the apostles were, and how sad it made them in their hearts that Jesus was going. But yet, he was going, and he reassured them that his going forth was an advantage for them and not a disadvantage. And we too, living now, 2,000 years later can sometimes ask ourselves the same question. Is the invisibility of Christ a disadvantage or an advantage? Is the fact that Jesus sits at the right hand of the Father an advantage to us or a disadvantage to us?

We need to enter here for a moment into the mystery of what this feast is all about. It is one of the great feasts of the Church. We speak about the Lord who goes up with a blare of trumpets. Clearly the spirit of the Church in this moment is the spirit of Jesus. We take it that it's an advantage and that today is a good feast, not a bad feast, because we celebrate it with joy.

So, what is at the very core of this feast? Well, I would like to propose to you an analogy. This little parable is about ambassadors. You know that governments send ambassadors to one another. For example, our government is sent a British ambassador so that we might have access to the Prime Minister of Britain. We have our U.S. ambassador over in London. Rather than try and get the Prime Minister on the phone, our ambassador goes and makes representation to ensure that the British government is always aware of our needs and our desires. So it's about access. We also know, from the news more recently, the way people pay for access is by making big donations to the right causes. They seek access. We could understand this mystery of the ascension as an event by which Christ gives us universal access to the Godhead, to God himself. By ascending and taking his rightful place at the right hand of the Father, we have Jesus there with us. And remember that it isn't just Jesus' soul or his divinity that ascended to the right hand of the father. It was Jesus himself, Jesus Christ, Jesus of Nazareth, true God and true man, the same one who was born of the Blessed Mother in Bethlehem. That one person, that single person with his two natures now sits at the right hand of the father. Jesus being there is our presence. Through Jesus our humanity is present there with the Father. So, in some sense the ascension brings to its radical summit the mystery of the Incarnation. Because now Jesus of Nazareth sits at the right hand of the Father, and all power is given to him.

In the letter to the Ephesians, Saint Paul is already dealing with this issue. It is clear in the experience of the Church, even if they weren't able to understand why. By the time Saint Paul writes this letter, it is clear that when Jesus left this world and could no longer be encountered on the dusty roads of Palestine, instead of becoming weaker or dissipating, the Church became stronger, more vital, and more vigorous. When Jesus ascended to the Father, the Church continued to grow. People's lives continued to be changed by the grace of Christ and by the action of Christ. It was very clear to Saint Paul that Christ lives and that Christ is active and living in the Church.

The Feast of the Ascension by its very nature is in some way part one of a two-parter. Maybe there's some TV show you watch, and in one episode, when you are waiting for the story to end, it says, "To be Continued." You say, "Ah. I have to wait another week to see how this story ends." Well, the Feast of the Ascension is the first part of a two-parter. Next Sunday we will see revealed in its fullness the way in which Christ remains present for the world. The dynamic. Indeed, I think it can be clearly seen, and I think that perhaps we can intuit Jesus' intention. Instead of having Pentecost happen a few hours after the Ascension, or immediately after the Ascension, he tells his apostles to stay in Jerusalem and wait. Don't leave the city but wait. Those days, which we'll celebrate in this coming week, were for the apostles a time in which Jesus had ascended to the Father and the Holy Spirit had not yet descended upon them. Jesus gave them those days to highlight the power of the Holy Spirit. They would highlight the new life that lives in the Church, by the power of the Holy Spirit.

As we reflect this week on that period between the Ascension and Pentecost, we will see that the apostles, full of faith, full of trust in Jesus, prayerful in everything, were still entirely dominated by the world. They were still full of fear. In fact, Pentecost takes place with the apostles in the upper room with the doors barred.

Jesus is preparing something great for us. His ascension to the right hand of his Father is a vital part of what he is preparing for us. At the right hand of the Father, he looks upon the world with love. Not one of us becomes remote from him. Neither through time, history, or geography are we apart from him. We are a thousand years separated from Christ; we're 9,500 miles distant from Palestine, but yet we're not separated from him. And perhaps, who knows, in the future we may go off planet, and we still won't be more distant from him. When our astronauts are walking on Europa, or when they are voyaging to Alpha-Centauri or wherever, they won't be more distant from God than any one of us is now. So, neither time nor space get between us and our relationship with God and Jesus Christ our Savior. This is why he ascends to the right hand of the Father, so that he will be with every one of us always.

The biggest proof of this unity is sanctity. In this short period of our lives, we have known people, on our television screens or maybe even in the flesh, who are already canonized saints in heaven. Perhaps some of you were in Cherry Creek State Park in 1993, or in Mile High Stadium or one of the other venues where John Paul II came. He is now a saint in heaven. Saint John Paul II. Just like Saint Paul, Saint Augustine, Saint

Benedict, Saint Thomas, or Saint Ignatius to pick saints throughout these 2,000 years. Sanctity is a fruit of Christ's redeeming grace. The fact that there are saints in every age shows the very way in which this Church, this reality, works. It shows that this discipleship of Christ, that Christ set up, works. His ascension to the right hand of his Father, which is structurally essential to His setting up of the Church with His call to discipleship, really does work. As I have so often said to you, there is not a single person here not called to that holiness and sanctity. We are all called to be a saint ourselves. It is enough that we admit him entirely and totally, without fear or reservations, to our soul, and we will be saints. Who knows if we'll be recognized in the calendars of the Church? Recognition is not necessary, but sanctity is necessary. The fruits of sanctity continue to abound, right up to our own very times, 2,000 years later.

In one final comment, just look around you in the Church tonight. We're all here 2,000 years later. Five hundred people or more gathered this morning at 9:30 AM around the altar for the Eucharist. Is Christ alive or not? Of course he is. Christ is alive. Christ is present; Christ is here. Let us then thank the Lord for the gift of his abiding presence in this mysterious humanity, the human companionship which we call the Church.

May 24, 2015
Pentecost

READINGS

First Reading: Acts of the Apostles 1:1-11
Second Reading: Ephesians 4:1-13
Gospel Reading: Mark 16:15-20

COLLECT

Graciously hear our supplications, O Lord, so that we, who believe that the Savior of the human race is with you in your glory, may experience, as he promised, until the end of the world, his abiding presence among us. Who lives and reigns with you in the unity of the Holy Spirit, one God, for ever and ever.

The Gift of Restored Order

Brothers and sisters in Christ, today we celebrate the great event of the birth of the Church. Today's readings help us to understand this vital step that Pentecost is in the birth of the Church. We don't recognize the birth of the Church in Jesus' death on the cross. We don't recognize the birth of the Church even in his resurrection from the dead. We recognize the birth of the Church in this, the great Feast of Pentecost. The Church is born in coming of the Holy Spirit on the apostles and the enlivening of the Christian community with a new and vital life to which you and I belong now. We belong to that same life, still vibrant 2,000 years later.

Over the last weeks I have asked you to just look around you and see this full Church that is gathered here around this altar. Our presence is the manifestation of the Holy Spirit. It is by the power of the Holy Spirit that across this gap of 2,000 years that now separate us from the last time Jesus physically walked the streets of our earth, we are gathered here in his presence. Despite those thousands of miles that separate us from the Holy Land, by the power of the Holy Spirit we are gathered here in his presence, with him present, and as his presence. And that, my friends, is the mystery whose birth we celebrate today.

As we have often meditated, five minutes before the Holy Spirit came the apostles were in that upper room, full of fear. The doors were barred from the inside, and they were not out announcing anything to anyone. The prospective for this new little community of Jesus' followers was fairly grim. If those few chosen by Jesus as the pillars of his new community were locked in an upper room with the doors barred from the inside, what was going to happen in 20; 50; 100; 1,000; 2,015 years? The prospective were not very good. All of that changed radically with the Pentecost event – the coming of the Holy Spirit on the apostles. At the moment those doors were thrown open, a great mission in the world began. This event is the beginning of the epoch of the Church, the beginning of the life of the Church.

Already we hear in the first and second readings the vitality of this community that sprang from that fear and received the gifts of the Holy Spirit. Could I ask that any kids who were confirmed here a couple of weeks ago put up their hands for a moment? You received the Holy Spirit; this Pentecost event continues and lives in the world. That is what we celebrate today.

In a very brief theological synthesis, Jesus tells us in the Gospel that when the Holy Spirit comes, he will lead you to all truth. We could summarize "all truth" in that mysterious, tiny but powerful four-letter word that we speak about so much: love. Ultimately, as was explained to the confirmandi at our confirmation Mass, the kernel of the truth that the Holy Spirit comes to remind us is that God is love. God reveals himself as love, and indeed he even reveals the very content of the word *love*. That content is the life to which we are invited, that life of Christ in the world, recognized by the power of the Holy Spirit, and present by the power of the

Holy Spirit. The meaning of the word *love* is the life of this reality that we call the Church.

Today's theme, however, is not a reflection on that love, as we have done that many times, and no doubt we'll do it again and again. As Saint Teresa of Avilla said, all of prayer and contemplation is ultimately a pondering of the content of that one little word: *love*, the discovery, and the opening up in Christ of that little word *love*. However, that's for another day.

Today, I'm charged by our Bishop to introduce to you an initiative that he has decided to take for the archdiocese of Denver. As we were celebrating the conclusion of those forty Paschal days after his resurrection, when Jesus lived in the world with his apostles and then ascended into heaven, I explained that in some way, somewhat humorously, it's a two-parter. It's like one of those episodes you watch on television, and when you are expecting the next step in the narrative, it says "To be continued." And you have to wait a whole week to see what comes next. Well, we've waited a week now since the ascension of Jesus into heaven, and today comes the second part of Jesus' plan for the salvation of the world. Now comes the birth of the Church and the way in which Jesus is going to be present for the rest of history, to reach us – each one of us.

Today I want to introduce another two-parter. We should actually even say a three-parter because the sacraments of initiation are the sacraments by which we, when we are born and grow to adulthood, receive from Christ the fullness of life. These three sacraments are the sacraments that make up what we call Christian initiation. They are Baptism, Confirmation, and Eucharist. This is the order in which we've always named these sacraments, because this is the historic order in which these sacraments took place. The initiative I am speaking about today is what the bishop calls the restoration of the order of the sacraments of initiation.

How did the sacraments of initiation get out of order? Well, they got out of order in a very casual and innocent way. Pope Saint Pius X, who reigned as pope at the very beginning of the 1900's, desired that the Christian community be nourished more deeply and more profoundly by the Eucharist. Back then it was very common to receive the Eucharist only once a year. We know that one of the precepts of the Church says that you must receive the Eucharist worthily once a year. Well in many places it had been reduced to that once a year and the young people did not receive the Eucharist until much later in life. Pope Pius X insisted on the frequent reception of the Eucharist, a tradition that happily has now become the tradition of the whole Church. He also insisted on the reception of the Eucharist by the young as soon as they were able to have any real understanding of what that sacrament was. This is what became known in the Church as reaching the *age of reason*. In this way communion was brought to a much younger age, to about seven years old, which seemed to be the age at which that minimum of reason came to understand the mystery of the Eucharist. When a child understood that the white host was not just a piece of bread but that it was really Christ, it signaled the age of reason.

Therefore, communion was moved to age seven, but confirmation got left until later in life and was out of sync.

Already in the documents of the Second Vatican Council, written over fifty years ago now, is this idea that these sacraments should be restored to their original order. But time has gone by and it hasn't happened in many places. In some it has, but in many places it hasn't. Well, what the bishop wants to communicate today, on this Pentecost Sunday, is that here in the diocese of Denver, over the next five years, we are going to begin to bring Confirmation back into its proper place, before the reception of Holy Communion.

Confirmation and Baptism really are a two-parter. A very strong analogy can be drawn between the relationship of Easter to Pentecost and the relationship of Baptism to Confirmation. In some way Easter contains everything within it, but Jesus' resurrection from the dead is the definitive victory. That feast is nonetheless crowned, completed, and brought to effect through the Feast of Pentecost, and the Church is born. As I say, we grow on the tree whose seeds sprouted for the first time on that Pentecost Sunday and brought to us the Easter gifts. It's the same with the sacrament of Confirmation. In Baptism we already receive the life of God in our souls. The Holy Spirit already comes to us. The Trinity dwells in us: Father, Son, and Holy Spirit. But our baptism then gets crowned, confirmed, and brought to its fullness in another great sacrament, which is the sacrament of confirmation; the sacrament of the coming of the Holy Spirit, with his wondrous gifts.

Both of these sacraments, then, which are sacraments that leave an indelible seal, that are received only once, are in some way the gateway sacraments to the fullness of the life of the Church. What is the fullness of the life of the Church but the Eucharistic life? So, these two sacraments usher us into the Eucharistic life. And what should flow directly from these two sacraments, baptism and confirmation, is that Eucharistic life – in our first Holy Communion, and then all the communions that follow for the remainder of our life.

When we say Baptism, Confirmation, and Eucharist, we don't just mean first Eucharist. We mean all the Eucharists that we will receive throughout our whole life. When we talk about the sacrament of the Eucharist we mean the life of relationship with Christ in the Eucharist that sustains and is at the very heart of Catholic life. What are we initiated into by Baptism and Confirmation? We are initiated into Eucharist, and into the Eucharistic life, which is the life of the Church. As you can see, these three sacraments are inextricably linked. The bishop simply wants to bring back to us the strength and the force of that dynamic of God's grace at work.

There are two other reasons, that I will mention briefly for which the bishop wants to take this initiative. One is the fact that our children today have truly become a battleground between the secular world and the love of Christ that lives in the family. It is a battle that is intransigent. The secular world will never remit, will never give quarter, will never cease in its endeavor to be the determining factor in the life of our children. What stands in front of that is the edifice of faith and the edifice of life in Christ. The edifice of the life of grace stands as a bulwark against the world. That life of grace comes precisely from these sacraments. So, another reason for this restoration is that it gives to our young people the power of this extraordinary grace of Confirmation and the gifts of the Holy Spirit. When this battle for the souls, for the hearts of our young people enters its most decisive phase, the fruit that the Holy Spirit produces empowers the lives of those who receive him.

The third reason for which the Bishop would like to restore this sacrament is to be a great and strong support for family life. It's a clear thing to Catechists and to people who study the religious journey of a human being from infancy to adulthood that a religious education program that takes place one hour a week in your parish church is of absolutely no avail without the profound faith commitment of the family. Only the family that is living the faith with profound commitment really ends up producing children of faith. People need to see – to be convinced you need to see. People aren't going to accept Christianity because it has existed for 2,000 years, or because its ideas are lovely. People will adopt Christianity because it is convincing, and because they see its life. But this life must be seen in the home. Therefore, the Bishop wants to give this gift to the family as well. This full initiation of our children in that younger age is a gift to support and strengthen the family as they venture forward in the great and challenging adventure of educating their children in the faith.

The Bishop explains all this in a pastoral letter which he produced; it is available as of today. It's called *Saints Among Us; Restored Order of the Sacraments of Initiation: A Pastoral Letter from Archbishop Samuel J. Aquila.*[10] I truly invite you to read this letter. Especially those families who are engaged in those years of the formation of their children, and the initiation of their children in the Christian life, you really ought to read this.

Why change? Change is not easy for any of us. Change is always a little bit difficult. On the other hand, that which is alive will always change. That which is dead is the only thing that doesn't change. That which is inanimate does not change. That which is alive always changes. All we need to do is look in the mirror, and we'll see, we who are alive change, right? Our hair goes to grey, and wrinkles appear. We change. Change is a sign of life. If you want to truly understand the reasons for what's happening, I really beg you to read the Bishops letter. It's all there. So, let us go forward on this adventure. It's a five-year program. It's not going to shake up the lives of anyone immediately. But it is an adventure on which we are embarking. It will involve particularly our school and our religious education department.

I want to leave you with one final image. Normally we have an order in which things happen. You graduate high school, you learn to drive, you graduate college, you go get a job, and you get married, right? Now just suppose the step of learning to drive kind of got put out of place, and you didn't learn to

---

[10] Archdiocese of Denver, "Saints Among Us," https://saintsdenver.com/

drive until you were thirty. It would make things awkward. What if the step of learning to drive was moved and now you could get your driver's license at age fifteen and a half? People would say, "Oh, wow. Finally, good. Someone's putting it right again." We need to recognize in this gift of the sacrament of Confirmation to our younger children, that it is something to our advantage, not a burden of change, but a gift of grace. That's the way the Bishop wants to present it to us.

June 2, 2019
The Ascension of the Lord

READINGS

First Reading: Acts of the Apostles 1:1-11
Second Reading: Ephesians 1:17-23
Gospel Reading: Luke 24:46-53

COLLECT

Gladden us with holy joys, almighty God,
and make us rejoice with devout thanksgiving,
for the Ascension of Christ your Son
is our exaltation,
and, where the Head has gone before in glory,
the Body is called to follow in hope.
Through our Lord Jesus Christ, your Son,
who lives and reigns with you in the unity of the Holy Spirit,
one God, for ever and ever.

Jesus' Exit Strategy

Today is one of the great feasts: the Ascension of the Lord. It is probably one of the four greatest feasts in the Church's year, along with Christmas, Easter, and Pentecost. The Lord's ascension into heaven is one of the great feasts very strongly linked to Pentecost because it is the way the Lord Jesus predisposes his Church for us. The same Church in which we are now gathered around the altar. Jesus had this Church in mind when he decided on, what I guess in very modern terms you could call, his "exit strategy." After his wondrous incarnation, his life in the world, his passion, his death, his resurrection, and his showing himself to many people, his exit strategy would be the way he decided to terminate this process.

Yet Jesus does not terminate it at all; rather he makes it in some way permanent. He did this so that you and I, in 2019, could be beneficiaries of what he did, and of his life, and of his gift, just as much and as strongly as those who were in that room when he appeared after his resurrection. He wants us to benefit just as much as those who were in that room when the Holy Spirit came upon the apostles at Pentecost and as those who were with him, gathered around looking up to heaven when he ascended to the right hand of his father. He did not want us to lose out by the centuries that separate us from those events themselves. That is what he has done.

There is a very interesting thing that happens here in the Gospel and it is worth noticing. We all know who Jesus is, we have the crucifix, and we have statues of him all over the place. We kind of have an idea of the heavenly Father. Maybe it is an image of this old, white haired, bearded man who looks on us with tenderness and love. Maybe we have the image of the Father in the ceiling of the Sistine Chapel. We have a sense of who the Father is. What about the Holy Spirit? A dove? A kind of white pigeon? Does that really help you to understand who the Holy Spirit is? Maybe not, but today's Gospel really does. What is going to happen over the next week, in the liturgical life of the Church, also helps us. We need to understand deeply that the Holy Spirit is not, as some people have said, the forgotten person of the Trinity. The Holy Spirit is powerfully active in the Church. I always point this out because I think it is very important for us to notice, what does Jesus do? Jesus says: "I am ascending to the Father." He also says that the apostles should stay in the city. He tells them to wait, because he is going to send them the Father's gift. That gift is the Holy Spirit and that is what we will celebrate next week.

Yet this week is important too. What happens during this week? We have the apostles who have seen the risen Lord; they have eaten with him, they have talked with him, they have heard him speak to them about many things, and they have received from him the commission to go out and preach the Gospel to the whole world. They have received it all. Yet they are not doing it. One of things you will notice if you read the Acts of the Apostles is that they are still paralyzed by fear. In fact, on Pentecost Sunday, they are not out on a mission to build the Church. They are not out preaching or gathering in the temple area after a long day of announcing the Gospel to the people. The apostles are in the Upper Room. They are still in that room where they ate the Last Supper with the Lord. They are still in that room that Jesus entered even though the doors were closed. Those doors are still closed and barred. I believe that Jesus told them to wait in Jerusalem. He made them wait twelve whole days after his ascension before he gave them the Holy Spirit so that they would know that to make the Church grow was not in their power. He wanted them to know it was not their ability to preach, not their genius or wonderful personalities that are what make the Church grow, but it is precisely this gift of the Holy Spirit. He is the one who makes the Church grow. The Spirit is the one who makes the Church live. He is the one who touches human hearts by allowing them to see Christ's presence in the life of the Church.

We have commented many times that every Easter we receive new people into the Church who did not meet Jesus on the dusty roads of Palestine, but rather met Jesus here, among us. Believing by meeting other Christians is the work of the Holy Spirit, and it is powerful work. We are still here, 2,000 years later. We are still gathered around the altar celebrating him. We are still drawing life from and encountering Christ. We still find life in that encounter, and this is the work of the Holy Spirit. So, the Holy Spirit isn't invisible. We just need to know how to look for him. We need to know how to recognize his awesome power in our midst because he is the one who grants holiness. He is the one who gives us and the Church life. He is the one who makes the Church more than the sum of its parts. Even now we can think of some of the difficulties and the scandals that have occurred in the life of the Church. If the Church was just this sum of the parts, well, I don't know how good a thing that would be right now. Yet it is not the sum of the parts. It is a body that has a life of its own, given by the Spirit, that allows Jesus to be available and encountered by you and me always.

Now, if Jesus had stayed in the world and we weren't celebrating the Ascension today, we would not be able to have that open relationship with him that is complete, total, and available to each and every one of us always. Jesus ascended to the right hand of his Father, not to distance himself from us, but so that this new epoch in the life of the world could begin. This new epoch we call the epoch of the Church. Jesus goes to the Father so that we can all be in relationship with him through the power of the Holy Spirit. Throughout the entire life of the Church we call on the Holy Spirit to make Christ present. You will notice if you pay attention to the parts of the Mass that the consecration is the moment in the Mass that gives us Jesus in the Eucharist. Before the consecration of the Mass there is only bread and wine. After the consecration of the Mass, Christ is sacramentally present, really present here for us. How does that happen? The priest says,

> Lord, send your spirit upon these gifts that they may become for us the body and blood of Christ.

This is called the *Epiclesis* and it means the coming down of the Holy Spirit; it's the invocation of the Holy Spirit. This invocation is in every sacrament. For example, when the priest hears your confession and says the long version of the absolution, which I always do, he holds his hand over your head, and he calls the Holy Spirit. By the power of the Holy Spirit he communicates to you the forgiveness of your sins, which is the gift of Christ through his passion, death, and resurrection. So, we can see at work in the sacraments the very same dynamic that is also working continually in the life of the Church: the Holy Spirit. Christ goes to the Father and sits at the right hand of the Father so that he is available to you and me. Always. Continually. Now. There is no advantage to going back 2,000 years. There is no advantage to going to the Holy Land, although it is beautiful, and I recommend it. It's a wonderful boost for your faith to see the very places where these scenes from the Gospel happen. Yet there is no rule. There is no pilgrimage that we have to do every year or even once in our life to the Holy Land. We don't need to do that because he is right here. Jesus is right here, right now, fully present and fully able to give us every gift that he has in store for us right now. There is no separation.

My friends, this is what we celebrate on the ascension of Jesus into heaven: he goes to bring his work to its completion and to make it so that we too, you and I, are blessed. It truly can be said without any doubt that as the Lord ascended into heaven, he was thinking of you and me; of our very faces. He was thinking of you and me, the very people that we are, not just generic people in 2019, but each and every one of us. It might seem too much for the mind of God, but the mind of God as you know is infinite. He loves individually, purposefully, and directly each one of us. This gift, this ascension into heaven, and his sending the Holy Spirit upon us, is the gift of his love for you and me. Let us rejoice in it.

June 7, 2015
The Solemnity of the Most Holy Body and Blood of Christ (Corpus Christi)

READINGS

First Reading: Exodus 24:3-8
Second Reading: Hebrews 9:11-15
Gospel Reading: Mark 14:12-16, 22-26

COLLECT

O God, who in this wonderful Sacrament have left us a memorial of your Passion, grant us, we pray, so to revere the sacred mysteries of your Body and Blood that we may always experience in ourselves the fruits of your redemption. Who live and reign with God the Father in the unity of the Holy Spirit, one God, for ever and ever.

An Architectural Sacrament

This feast that we celebrate today stands at the center of the very life of the Church, because the Eucharist is the center of the life of the Church. Today, rather than share many thoughts with you, I invite you to a participation in the procession that we're going to have after the Mass. I'm just going to make a few short points here so that we can have the time we need for our procession. We can think of this as a homily in action as we follow the Lord through the streets of our town. We'll walk down just a few streets, but they are symbolic of our whole city, into which we, through our reception of the Eucharist, bring the living Lord every time we come here on Sunday. This little procession of ours is an explicative gesture that expresses something much, much bigger. It expresses that mission that the Eucharist generates in us, as Jesus shares his life with us and sends us out as his feet, mouth, ears, and hands into the world to bring the mystery of his love.

There is a brief idea I would like to share with you today that comes from the great theologian von Balthasar.[11] When reading the Gospel of Matthew, von Balthasar noticed something unusual. We know that Matthew's Gospel is the earliest, and is considered by the theologians the least redacted, the least composed of the Gospels, and therefore the one in which it is most likely that we would find what they

[11] The Swiss theologian Hans Urs von Balthasar (1905 – 1988) is among the theologians of the twentieth century whose significance has endured.

call the *Ipsissima Verba Jesu*—"the very words of Jesus himself." In this little dialog with the apostles, in which Jesus is sending them to prepare the place for the celebration of the Last Supper, we find that Jesus has already made the arrangements. When they go there, the apostles will find a room in which everything has already been prepared for the Last Supper. What von Balthasar points out here is that this is the way it is for us at Mass, too. When we come to Mass, it's not what we bring, but it's what we find already waiting for us. That's the pearl of great price, that's the thing of value here.

As I said in the introductory comment, we come to the Church, ourselves, our families, our friends, all the various people with which whom we share life in this community, to gather in these pews, and around this altar. As Jesus gives himself to us on this altar in the Eucharist, something extraordinary happens. This community – it becomes more than the sum of its parts. There is something here that infinitely transcends the sum of its parts, even while being us. This is the mystery of the Church. This is the mystery of the people of God that, fed by the living bread of the Eucharist, and living in the communion of the Church, we become something that transcends infinitely what we simply are, left to our own devices. God catches us up in the great and immense story of love, which is the very life of the Trinity itself and makes us a part of that. Therefore, we live in the world, not just as a whole series of natural relationships that we try to live as best as we can, but as the very living presence of God in the world. We live as the presence of Christ continuing to live in the world.

This, my friends, is the work of the Eucharist. The Eucharist in the life of the Church is what we might call an architectural sacrament. This reminds me of when I saw a place in the basement where there is an immense column, one of the four columns supporting the whole roof of this church. The columns are immense, But we don't see them. Well, when I say that the Eucharist is an architectural sacrament, I mean this: it is the sacrament that edifies and holds aloft this whole reality, this transcendent reality of faith. This reality is the Church, on its now over 2,000-year journey through the history of the world. We bring the Lord himself to every corner of the world, to every person in the most distant tribes and villages, and to the greatest cities of our civilization today. Following the Vatican council, we always say this Eucharist is the beating heart that pumps the blood of life into the body.

We must never take the Eucharist for granted. We must always stand in wonder, amazement, and ultimately in adoration, on front of this extraordinary gift which the Lord gives to us today. The beauty of our Mass, the beautiful music which has been prepared for us, the beautiful songs of our tradition that we will sing, are all to give us an opportunity to express that adoration, wonder, and praise. These traditions are given to educate us to an attitude that becomes an integral part of our Catholic life. Let us rejoice, then, in this wonderful gift as we go together in celebration.

June 9, 2019
Pentecost Sunday

READINGS

First Reading: Acts of the Apostles 2:1-11
Second Reading: 1 Corinthians 12:3B-7, 12-13
Sequence: Veni, Sancte Spiritus
Gospel Reading: John 20:19-23

COLLECT

Almighty ever-living God,
who willed the Paschal Mystery
to be encompassed as a sign in fifty days,
grant that from out of the scattered nations
the confusion of many tongues
may be gathered by heavenly grace
into one great confession of your name.
Through our Lord Jesus Christ, your Son,
who lives and reigns with you in the unity of the Holy Spirit,
one God, for ever and ever.

Purification of Desire

Today we celebrate with great joy the birth of the Church that Christ constituted. The Church saw its vibrant life born on the first Pentecost Sunday. Before the Holy Spirit came, the apostles lived in their world of fear as the Jews that kept them captive. The apostles were living most of their lives still locked in that upper room, where they had been when Jesus appeared to them after his resurrection. There they were, in the same room where they had celebrated the Last Supper, much of their time spent there in fear. Now with the Holy Spirit coming in power, all of a sudden, instead of fear the Church is born. A new reality comes into the world and the Gospel begins to be announced as we just heard in the reading from the Acts of the Apostles. They are out in the street corners announcing the Gospel. If we read through the whole book of the Acts of the Apostles, which we've done in the liturgy these last few weeks, we see the beautiful unrolling story of the birth of our Church. We hear the story of this very same Church that gathers us here this morning in worship around the altar, the center of the life of the Church. The Church is vivified by the Holy Spirit. *Vivified* means it is given life; it receives its life from the Holy Spirit.

This life, what sort of a life is this? What is the Church? Sometimes when we think of the Church, we think of the great institutions that are in the service of the life of the Church. We think of St. Peter's square, the Vatican, the pope, our archbishop, and maybe even the external trappings of the

Church. However, all of these things are in the service of a life, because first and foremost the Church is a life. A life of grace. A life that is truly life. Jesus himself used this word life to express the nature of the gift that he came to give. "I came so that you might have life, and to have it to the full." (John 10:10) Ultimately the Church is this life and it is served by these great institutions, the sacraments that are instituted in order to serve its life.

Jesus gave us the authority of Peter so that we could be guided on our way. Jesus ordained his apostles so that we could always have the proclamation of the truth and the gift of the Eucharist. Above all, today we celebrate the sending of this extraordinary gift of the Holy Spirit upon the Church. This gift of the Holy Spirit is the gift of the one who makes us holy.

Now I want to concentrate for a few minutes on this call to holiness. It was considered one of the great accomplishments of the Second Vatican Council. Up until then, it was sometimes conceived that perhaps only priests, monks, nuns, and these sorts of people were called to holiness, but the general population in the pew were called to something less. This was never the teaching of the Church. When the Second Vatican Council proclaimed the universal call to holiness, they were taking it from deep within the tradition of the Church. The Church always understood and taught that each and every one of us, in whatever form of life we live, is called to holiness. There was even a tradition of calling the religious orders institutes of perfection.

Yet each of us is an institution of perfection. Marriage is an institution of perfection. Baptism is the institution of perfection. Jesus said to us, be perfect, as your heavenly Father is perfect. That was not an invitation to any particular group or leadership, but it was an invitation to every single human soul. This is what is powerfully signified by the fact that on that Pentecost Sunday, as we heard in the first readings, there were people from all around the world, and each one heard them speaking in a way that they could understand, in their own language. This event suggests the destination of this new life that Christ came to bring. When the Holy Spirit ignites the life of the Church, we know it is a gift for each and every one. There is no place or person who is not destined to this vocation and is not called by this great call. There is no person who is not invited by this invitation to be perfect as our heavenly Father is perfect.

What we need to understand is this: the Holy Spirit is the one who carries out this work in our life. One of the titles of the Holy Spirit is that he is the Sanctifier. What is this work? And what is this holiness? What does holiness look like? First of all, we always need to understand that the one who is holy is not the one who is exalted or is in some way separated out. We have this idea of the saint on a pedestal that is so far above us we cannot even dream of that life for ourselves. The work of John Paul II and the popes that have followed him, Pope Benedict and Pope Francis now, have helped with this by speeding up the process of canonization. We have people who are saints and who we remember well: Mother Teresa of Calcutta and John Paul II, just to name two. These people were already saints and have been to our city of Denver, Colorado. These saints have been among us and have touched the very life of our community. There are probably several people here who were present in 1993 when Saint John Paul II came among us on that wonderful occasion of World Youth Day. So, saints are not so separate from us as we might think, and each one of us is called to holiness.

What is holiness? In the end, holiness is a very, very simple thing. Paul describes it well here in the Letter from Saint Paul to the Romans. I really commend Saint Paul to you to study. It is hard to grasp a reading of Saint Paul when it's read out once on Sunday in a crowded church. You need to sit down with Saint Paul and maybe even with a commentary or a good dictionary of the Bible and start to follow it through. Let's just touch the surface of the letter because the surface touches exactly the key message of today's feast: this universal call to holiness. Each one of us has to say, "Who is called to holiness?" Me. I am called. Each one of us is called to holiness. That is what I am called to, and that is where we begin; it is the life that God is giving us. Holiness is a response to God. In the end, that's what holiness is. It's the response of our life to God. It's the relativity of our life to God. It's the fact that we place that relationship with God before everything else in our lives.

We are very good at planning. We make projects, set goals, and determine what projects we would like to work on and how we would like them to turn out. We are very good at imagining the future of our own life and having a clear idea about what our expectations for life are. Yet I have to tell you that if we live only like this, then we are entirely living what Saint Paul is calling here, living in the flesh. As he says, it is truly empty. In the end it has nothing to give us. No matter how great the goals we accomplish, if they are goals that we set for ourselves, they are ultimately of no avail to who we are as human beings, to our hearts, to who God made us to be. We are made for relationship with God. You and I are infinite in the dimension of our soul: of our heart, of what it is for which we are made. We are made for relationship with him. This is what holiness looks like: a certain detachment from our own schemes, our own ideals, our own goals. By that I don't mean not having goals, aims, and objectives in life, but we need to be detached from them.

What does being detached from them mean? It means that there is something more vital to me than the accomplishment of this goal, and that is the will of God. Being detached means living the will of God: living for him; living the relationship with him always and intensely. All the projects and goals that we might have in life only contribute to our humanity, to our life, to our joy, to us being full of life. Our personal goals contribute to our humanity in as much as they are within this "yes" to God, this adhering to the will of God. We are made for adhesion to his will. Happiness comes from that will. Joy and fulfillment come from that will.

When I say we have to do the will of God, maybe there is an instinctive little rebellion in the soul somewhere that says, "Why his will? Why not my will? What happens to my will? What about me? If I do the will of God will I be crushed? If I do the will of God, what will happen?" Here is where we have to go deeper. Unless we go deeper, we get the completely wrong idea about our relationship with God. The truth is that our humanity is made for that relationship with him. Therefore, it is only in that relationship with him that we really accomplish what it is we want. It's good sometimes to sit down and do what I call the meditation of the purification of desire. What you do is this: you make the sign of the cross, sit in a comfortable seat, and start to think, "What do I want?" Maybe right away you begin with the most superficial things. Yet if you sit there for a little while and begin to really think, "What is it that I really want?" you realize that it is not a Caribbean cruise, or everything else you might think you want. You realize that it is none of those things. The more you sit with this question, the more you will realize that what you want is exactly to be in communion with God because it's written in your nature. The other things disappear very quickly when we give ourselves the silence and the time to realize that. It is written so loudly and so profoundly in our hearts that we know it already.

These last few weeks, one of the things I have been busy with is going to different parishes doing confirmations on the Bishop's behalf. Something I always do with the confirmation is to draw this analogy between that great movie *The Incredibles*[12] and Confirmation. I talk to the kids about the secret powers that these superheroes have in this movie. We talk about how the heroes are not allowed to use their powers

[12] Brad Bird, director, *The Incredibles* (Emeryville, CA: Pixar, 2004).

because the world has grown cold to their work. They know that when an emergency develops, the superheroes have to use their powers to save the world. Out of necessity, the superheroes begin to discover their powers again. The kids sometimes don't even know what those powers are, yet they have to start practicing with them. I tell the confirmandi that the gifts of the Holy Spirit are a little bit like those powers. They are special powers; those seven gifts of the Holy Spirit are special powers that God is going to give them at their confirmation. I tell them that the only way they are going to discover those powers is by putting them into practice and by living them out. The next thing I tell them is that a superhero can take a car and toss it across the city or grab an airplane out of the sky and put it on the ground if it's going to crash. The superheroes in this movie can do things like that, very powerful things, but what you are going to be able to do with your superpowers is more important than that. What you are going to be able to do is love. The gifts of the Holy Spirit are powers for love. Then a little bit later after I let that sink in, I ask them, so which do you think is a greater power? Is it greater to be able to pick up a car and throw it across the city, or to be able to love? I say, "Hands up, those who think it would be greater to love?" I promise you, in an instant every single hand goes up. To me that happens not because they have all learned the lesson that Catholics should say it's better to love than anything else. To me every hand goes up because it is written in their hearts. They know it. Those little kids, in all their innocence and in their baptismal life they are living, they know the answer to this. They know that we are made not for the satisfaction that comes from the realization of what we want. They know we are made for love, and love is another name for that life of union with God. That is what this feast is about: the pouring out of the Holy Spirit on the world.

In the Collect we prayed that God pours out upon the world that grace, which at the first preaching of the Gospel was poured out upon the world. Let us ask that the Holy Spirit again pour himself forth us so that we might know for what life we are made. Let us ask that we may not waste our time and ultimately wound our society by living for something less than that for which we are made. The more we participate in the world incorrectly, the more we make this world a valley of tears. It is only when we participate in the world for what we truly are that we raise up the world, lift up the world, and become the rebuilders of houses destroyed, as the prophet says. So, let us ask for this outpouring of the Holy Spirit, and let us receive it above all. Asking is preparing a disposition within our souls to receive, because there is no hesitation on God's behalf in sending us his spirit. Zero. So, asking is above all preparing a welcome reception for the gift. Let us have the courage to ask for that gift and to prepare our souls a place for its reception.

June 16, 2019
The Solemnity of the Most Holy Trinity

READINGS

First Reading: Proverbs 8:22-31
Second Reading: Romans 5:1-5
Gospel Reading: John 16:12-15

COLLECT

God our Father, who by sending into the world
the Word of truth and the Spirit of Sanctification
made known to the human race your wonderous mystery,
grant us, we pray, that in professing the true faith,
we may acknowledge the Trinity of eternal glory
and adore your Unity, powerful majesty.
Through our Lord Jesus Christ, your Son,
who lives and reigns with you in the unity of the Holy Spirit,
one God, for ever and ever.

The Non-Solitude of God

If we were having the school Mass this morning, I would probably ask the young ones, "What feast is it today?" All the hands would go shooting up and they would have lots of different answers, but I'm going to tell you the answer today: it's the Feast of Almighty God. That sounds a little bit funny to our ears because in some way all days are the Feast of Almighty God. However, in a very special way, this Trinity Sunday is the Feast of Almighty God in his very nature, in who God is, and what God is like. This is all expressed in the great celebration of today.

Let's start with the scriptural situation that we have here. In the Gospel we see Jesus talking, as he very often did, about the relationships in which he lives. We see Jesus talking about his father and the Spirit. In this revelation of Jesus we see him continually in relationship of obedience to his Father and hear him promise to send the Spirit. From this we arrive at our belief in the Trinity of God: the Father, the Son, and the Holy Spirit. Jesus says the Father and I are one. Right? Jesus also says that he will send you his Spirit and the Father will send you his Spirit, and in these we see this mysterious trinity of God. The Trinity of God is a mystery because we can't explain how God can be one in perfect unity and have a triune nature. If someone comes and says to you, "Hey, come over here now and I'll explain the Trinity to you," walk away because nobody can explain the Trinity to you. What we can do is explain what has been revealed to us about the Holy

Trinity. Even in the Old Testament they don't know God is Father, Son, and Holy Spirit. Yet there are very important glimpses of this reality revealed throughout the story of the Old Testament. Here in this reading from the Book of Proverbs we get a very strong hint that God is not alone. The reading talks about Wisdom being in the presence of God and delighting in everything that God was doing as he made Creation. Wisdom delights in the presence of God and was there when he made the earth and the seas, and we see this image of the state of God as being not alone.

That brings me exactly to what I wanted to talk to you about this morning, this non-solitude of God. This fact that God is relational is a profound and deep mystery. There is an old phrase in Latin, *nemo potest dare quod non habet*, which means *nobody can give what they don't have.* Here's the interesting thing, we all say that God is love. Saint John says it, Saint Paul says it, and most of our kids would say it if I asked them; they would know God is love. How could God be love if he was monadic? There has to be relationship for there to be love. Love is in relationship. Love is actually a relationship. This is the great mystery of God, that he is relationship. That becomes even deeper when we realize that we are created by him.

First of all, let's take a moment and think about being created by him. Why would God create us? We know that God is completely self-sufficient. He doesn't need anything. When you say that God wants, this indicates that there is something outside of God that would perfect him if he had it. There is no such a thing. For that reason, we say that God, the very concept and nature of God, even as the human mind can conceive the possibility of God, has to be not lacking anything. God has everything. So why did God make us? And this is a beautiful intuition that comes to us on this feast. God made us because of his nature. God is love and it is in his nature to love. We are an emanation; all of creation is an emanation of God's love. We are an initiative of God's love. For example, a husband and wife might say, "We love each other, we know each other, and that's enough." Therefore, they just kind of go through life presuming on one another's love. But love doesn't work that way. Love is communication. Therefore, there are gifts, gestures, caresses, and so many ways in which that love is expressed. We are an expression of God's love. Our existence, this world, this reality is an emanation that emerges from God's love. I know that's kind of deep, but it's also true.

We come out of God's love. One way we sometimes phrase it so that we can get our minds around it, God made us because he knew that when we existed, we would enjoy existing. After he had made us, we would have joy in that existence. This is a way of trying to understand what it means that we come from God's love. God's love is in this sense like all love, and our share in God's love is an uncontainable thing. That noncontainment is one of the ways in which we see and discover this reality of which we are a part.

Then we come to this other intuition which is very important: we are made in the image and likeness of God. First page of the Bible, we are made in the image and likeness of God. In the very design specification from which you and I are made, there is this relationality, this relational nature. We are also made for relationship. We are not made to be alone. In those same first pages of the Bible, we read that it is not good for man to be alone. Nature is made for each other. That is why love, community, and communion lie at the very heart of the Christian experience; because we are made for love. Christ came into the world precisely to reconcile us to that plan of the father: that we would love one another as he has loved us. We are made for this, and anything less is simply not adequate.

There is one more extraordinary word of Saint Paul in the readings that I want to point out to you. He is speaking to us about hope and he says, "Hope does not disappoint." I think that this word disappointment is a very important word to think about and meditate on a little bit. Unfortunately, it is an experience that we all know. Disappointment. I don't just mean that the gift you got for your birthday wasn't what you were hoping for. I mean a deeper and more generalized disappointment. We thought that life would be full and completely answer our cravings and yearnings and desires and hungers; what we are made for. When we live the relationship with one another and the world in a way that doesn't receive this gift of God's revelation, we find life disappointing. By God's gift of revelation I mean this second initiative of his love, which is the sending of his son into the world. At first it all seems promise. The younger people in the world may find it hard to relate to this idea of disappointment because everything is promise and possibility; I'm going to do this, I'm going to do that, I'm going to become this, and when I'm this I'll do this. Everything looks open and full of promise. But then life begins to take another direction, and we begin to realize it, sometimes expressed in these questions: "Is this all there is?" "Is this it?" "Is this what life is?" This experience of disappointment isn't something completely negative; we should consider it as a complaint. Disappointment is the complaint of our heart.

Our heart is made for something truly great, but when we offer it a hundred and one small satisfactions, in the end the heart begins to say, "No. I'm not getting what I want here." New cars, new houses, new gadgets, trips, all the things you can put on the list of the things with which we tend to fill our lives. What I'm looking for, what the human heart is looking for, isn't there. It is not among those things. It is in the life that Jesus comes to bring us, and that life is nothing other than our share in this life of the Trinity. Christ brings us to share in the life of the Trinity and to live this relationship because this is what God made humanity to be. God made humanity to be something beautiful.

Only when we set our hearts on something less than our relationship with him does life stop being beautiful, and this world becomes that valley of tears which we know it to be. We experience that disappointment of finding out that there is a lot here, but not what I'm looking for. What I'm looking for is given as a gratuitous gift in our relationship with Christ. That's what he came for and it is nothing less than that share in his life by which we can actually and truly live that command of Jesus; be perfect and love one another as he has loved us. That command was already available in the Old Testament and was clearly the goal it proposed. Love your neighbor as yourself. Here Jesus invites us to a whole other dimension where that will be fulfilled. Certainly the one who loves God and loves as God has loved us is going to love their neighbor. Perhaps they may even love their neighbor more than they love themselves. Maybe in discovering an ever-deeper love for who one's self truly is, that person discovers an ever deeper and more profound love and communion with their neighbor.

This is an invitation to share in the Trinitarian life, which we celebrate today. It unites us in that reality that we call communion. It's a special word. As you know, communion means the Eucharist. It's the word we use for the Eucharist, but it is also the word for the unity of the people of God. That unity in the making is only nurtured and only grows stronger in-as-much as each one of us embraces this gift of life from God. We must allow this gift of God, this gift that Christ came to bring to us, to become the very form of our lives, the very way that we live our lives. Then the world begins to become a beautiful place. This is how Christianity spread in the first centuries: by the beauty of it. We read it in the Acts of the Apostles that non-Christians said they wanted life like the Christians have it. Again, my friends, this is the only route that the Church will ever find to convert the world, to win the world to itself. The beauty of life only emerges when we receive, welcome, and build our lives upon the gift of the Trinitarian life that Christ has come to give to us.

So, as we celebrate the Trinity again today, let us ask that we may welcome, accept, and embrace this great life which has been given to us so that our hearts may sing, and that the world may see something beautiful and convincing. Let us ask for this grace.

ORDINARY TIME

January 14, 2015
Wednesday of the First Week in Ordinary Time

READINGS

First Reading: Hebrews 2:14-18
Gospel Reading: Mark 1:29-39

COLLECT

Attend to the pleas of your people with heavenly care, O Lord, we pray, that they may see what must be done and gain strength to do what they have seen. Through our Lord Jesus Christ, your Son, who lives and reigns with you in the unity of the Holy Spirit, one God, for ever and ever.

Seeing and Being Moved

So today, once again wearing the green vestments, we begin this journey of ordinary time. Those words, *ordinary time*, make it seem like it is something less. Everything else is special but this is ordinary. However, in Latin *ordinary* means *ordered*, or a time that is numbered. Indeed, there are thirty-four weeks of this ordinary time. And far from being ordinary, in the modern English sense of the word, this time is extraordinary. In these thirty-four weeks we get to watch Jesus in action. We get to watch how Jesus communicated, through his humanity, the presence of his divinity. This is how people came to recognize him as true God and true man. Through the events that take place during these thirty-four weeks, people came to see him, to know him, to recognize him, and to ask questions about his nature. People began to open their hearts to the final response that he would give ultimately through his resurrection. So, this is an important chapter in the liturgical life of the Church. A small part of it happens before Lent, then we resume ordinary time after Pentecost, and it leads us right up to the beginning of next year's Advent.

This is what we open today. We open ordinary time following yesterday's Feast of the Baptismal Jesus. Now Jesus is calling his first disciples to him. We know that this is not his first encounter with the people that he is calling. These men have already come to know Jesus and have formed a friendship with him. For example, we know that Andrew and his brother John spent an afternoon in Jesus's house after John the

Baptist pointed him out by the river Jordan. Now that they know Christ, next comes a special vocation. This is the moment of their vocation to be with Christ, to follow Christ, and to adhere to him. This is the moment that he would become the true pattern of their lives. Up until then he was an inspiring teacher, perhaps even the Messiah. Now he is someone who has called them to himself. In these thirty-four weeks of ordinary time we'll see the unfolding of this adventure which the apostles begin with Jesus today.

I want to also take a moment to comment on the Collect prayer of the Mass. The Collect has this quite extraordinary prayer: Grant that we might see what needs to be done, and we might have the strength to do it. When I read that, I can't help but remember a friend of ours in Uganda called Rose. A documentary has been made about her life and her mission. For a few weeks the documentary crew follows Rose and an artist from Italy who comes to Uganda to see all of the work she is doing. The artist gets into the car and squeezes in beside Rose who is driving around and seeing all the difficulties that the people of Uganda have to face. The artist sees all the poverty, the hardships, and the disease. With great enthusiasm and commitment, he says, "We've got to do something. We've got to do something about this." Now Rose is an African herself, born in Uganda. While driving the car she kind of smiles and looking at him sideways says, "I don't know if it's about having to do something, I think it's about seeing and being moved." As the whole documentary plays out, you see how those two threads of human response play out. The response of "We've gotta do something," and the response of "seeing and being moved." This prayer in the Collect today absolutely talks about seeing and being moved.

We might see what needs to be done, and we might have what it takes to do something about it; to act upon it. Completely based on the power of God's grace, we might also be moved to become a protagonist. Rose, with that simple intuition of seeing and being moved, creates a wonderful and beautiful work called The Meeting Point.[13] This is a place where people suffering from AIDS can come together in Uganda. It is like a club, a society, or a gathering. It's a communion of people suffering from AIDS who all get better, not by a miracle, but because they are all living their humanity well. They are faithful to the drug regimens and are doing so well that when the United Nations come around to do something about the disease, they don't even believe that these people have AIDS. The doctors from the United Nations submit the people at The Meeting Place to tests and find out that they do indeed have AIDS.

Let us pray that we might see what needs to be done. The Collect says, "And have the strength to do what they have seen." That strength comes from God, and that is why I call it a prayer. So let us ask as we celebrate this Mass and begin this ordinary time, that we make the Collect prayer our own. Let us ask that we might see what needs to be done and that from God we might receive the strength to do it.

---

[13] See Meeting Point International, http://meetingpoint-int.org/home/

January 31, 2016
Fourth Sunday in Ordinary Time

READINGS

First Reading: Jeremiah 1:4-5, 17-19
Second Reading: Corinthians 12:31-13:13
Gospel Reading: Luke 4:21-30

COLLECT

Grant us, Lord our God, that we may honor you with all our mind, and love everyone in truth of heart. Through our Lord Jesus Christ, your Son, who lives and reigns with you in the unity of the Holy Spirit, one God, for ever and ever.

The Authority of Love

We have three beautiful readings today. At first glance it may seem hard to find the connection between them. The connection is actually very strong and very clear. If we understand it, then it will help us to live in a world that isn't always our friend.

In the first reading we have the commissioning by God himself. "The word of the Lord came to me saying...," commissioning the prophet Jeremiah for his mission and giving him a real authority to preach and proclaim the prophecy of God. And with this authority, Jeremiah will live out his life and his vocation.

Then, in the Gospel, we have Jesus coming to his hometown to preach the good news. The immediate response to Jesus is the experience of a great attraction. They were amazed by the effectiveness of his words. They were surprised and drawn and attracted by his words. Some of the fathers of the Church interpret this as an underrating of Jesus' words. "Oh, oh, how nice, how nice. And now we'll just go away." I am not sure if that is exactly what is going on here. There's another interpretation that suggests that the Gospel writers only give us the very essentials of any story. And that in actual fact the people were touched and deeply moved by Jesus when he spoke. As we have often commented here, Jesus spoke with authority. This word *authority* contains the root word of *author* meaning the one who is at the origin. If you could interview William Shakespeare about some of the more difficult passages in his plays, you would get the right interpretation because he is the author. Well, here Jesus is the author of our humanity. As he speaks to these human beings, they feel a correspondence between the way Jesus talks and who they are. They feel a correspondence that warms their hearts, but in this particular moment it doesn't win them over. Instead they begin to question themselves. "This is just one of our people. Who does he think he is?" The Gospel doesn't record it in those exact words, but you can read it between the lines. They are thinking, "Who does he think he is to come along here and speak to us in these grandiose and beautiful terms?" And then they reject him. The crowd ends up trying to throw Jesus off the cliff in the town where he was born. This is probably the very first attempt on Jesus' life recorded in the Gospels.

Finally, we come to the second reading, which is the great and beautiful hymn of love. This hymn is read at many weddings and appropriately so, because what weddings have at their very center is love. Yet this hymn is also a proclamation of a way of living. As Saint Paul says, there are a lot of ways to try and live this life of ours but let me point to you a better way. Then he introduces the way of love. Now let me try and make the connection between all of these ideas. All of these excerpts are about the authority of love. It is a strange expression, *the authority of love*, but love really does have an authority. Love has an authority that allows a person to act in a way that's courageous, bold, and strong.

The one who loves isn't one who is completely dominated by sentimentality, but rather the one who loves is the one who is strong in goodness.

Perhaps we can think of Mother Teresa of Calcutta. Many people tried to persuade her just to be a good little nun and to go back to her convent and stay in her room and teach her kids. Yet she had the authority of love. Precisely because of that authority of love, Mother Teresa insisted, against the strongest odds and the opinions of many, to follow the call that she had received from God to love. Through that authority of hers, a great, great light shone for all the world. No one failed to see the extraordinary light of Mother Teresa of Calcutta when she lived in this world among us. Even in that non-Christian land where she carried out her mission, there were millions who attended her funeral. Her light really did shine, but it would not have been so without the authority of love.

Another example of someone like Mother Teresa of Calcutta that most of us have known, at least on our television screens, is Pope John Paul II. I don't know if you've ever seen his visit to Latin America, but you can probably find it on YouTube and it's fascinating. When Pope John Paul II was in Latin America, there were a lot of people supporting the Communist Party. These people wanted to organize a moment of opposition against John Paul II when he was visiting. For his part, Pope John Paul II wanted to announce love. It was the heart of his engagement with the culture of Latin America. So, he goes there, and he is on the big dais that they have prepared for him, separating him a bit from the crowds because everyone knows that there are tensions. Sure enough, when the pope gets up to speak, they all start yelling and screaming and shouting their slogans. Pope John Paul II tries a couple of times to speak, but he is always drowned out by the crowd. Finally, he gets behind that cross of his that he loved. (I don't know if you've ever noticed that Pope John Paul II loved to stand behind the cross with the figure of Jesus right in front of his nose.) As Pope John Paul II stood behind the cross, he yells at the very top of his voice, "Basta!" It is heard echoing three times throughout the whole crowd. Suddenly a stillness begins to come upon the crowd, and everyone goes quiet. Then the pope delivers a message that contributed greatly to real progress in the continent of Latin America. This moment was the beginning of a unity in a place where the ultra-rich and the proletariat were engaging in class warfare. That very speech became a mark of love and it produced much, much fruit in that land and in that continent. But without an authority that says, "No, love has to be heard," no one would have listened. It was the pope's authority that allowed him to say "Love has to be seen, love has to speak, and I will not be quiet. I will not withdraw because I have come to offer you love."

Now back to Jeremiah who is commissioned by God not to be afraid. Jeremiah is told that he will not be beaten or silenced because his mission is a mission of love, and therefore he receives that authority to face those who would try to push love down. Jeremiah has the authority to face those who say that love can't work or is weak. He can confront those who say we need something stronger than love in order to change the world. No, my friends, love alone is all we need. That is the core of today's second reading. Love alone is the way. It is the better way and there is no other successful way to make the world a better place than love.

To see this in action, we have Jesus himself in the Gospel. Jesus is love itself. Love made flesh. Love is standing there in the synagogue in person, in the very physical form of Jesus of Nazareth speaking his words of love. There people are being warmed and moved by his words of love. But then the political action takes over through the instrument of popular opinion. To make an analogy with our times, you might say the newspapers would print the popular opinion. The journalists, the commentators, all would be saying, "But... but..." Everyone gets lost in these "buts," and Jesus walks through their midst because he knows that nothing will stop him speaking about love. His cross is the ultimate victory of that love. It is raised upon the cross that he wins his victory. The true human victory is not the subjugation of people, but the unity of people in love. As Jesus says, "When I am raised upon the cross, I will draw all of you to myself." (John 12:32) He does indeed draw us to himself. So many are gathered here this afternoon, around his Eucharist and around his cross. Even 2,000 years later he continues to draw us to himself by the authority of his love.

We, who are baptized, each one of us, have within ourselves that same authority of love. What the Lord God said to the prophet Jeremiah is truer of you and I who are baptized than even of Jeremiah. In our baptism we received an anointing, each one of us, as priest, prophet, and king. Now we have the authority of love and we must not withdraw. We must not settle for anything less than love. When we do, it is too small. Then, my friends, life can't but be disappointing. It becomes disappointing in the very depths of our heart. No matter how great our triumphs and success are, if they are not of love, they are ultimately disappointing.

Let us ask that words of love may rain down upon us always from those who guide us. We could have commented on our beloved Pope Francis, another person who uses the authority of love. May we too always be governed by love. I said that we were anointed in our baptism as priest, prophet, and king. What does it mean we are anointed "king" in our baptism? It means that we are given the power to rule our lives and our affairs in love. If each one of us would truly take seriously that kingly dignity of our baptism, and truly rule our affairs in love, as Saint Paul ascribes, rather than by any other pattern, then the world would be a different place, my friends.

Let us ask as we celebrate our Mass that love may triumph among us, with all of its strength and its vigor to ennoble and redeem. Let us ask for this grace for ourselves and for one another.

June 21, 2015
Twelfth Sunday in Ordinary Time

READINGS

First Reading: Job 38:1, 8-11
Second Reading: 2 Corinthians 5:14-17
Gospel Reading: Mark 4:35-41

COLLECT

Grant, O Lord, that we may always revere and love your holy name, for you never deprive of your guidance those you set firm on the foundation of your love. Through our Lord Jesus Christ, your Son, who lives and reigns with you in the unity of the Holy Spirit, one God, for ever and ever.

Fatherhood

You have to feel a little bit for the apostles on that day, being tossed about in the storm and feeling that their boat was going down. They were probably very reluctant to disturb Jesus, but finally the panic and danger totally seized them, and they felt they had no option but to wake him up. And what do they get? A rebuke! This consideration can help us to understand that there is something very important that Jesus is teaching here. This is not just a small event in the life of Jesus. Something vitally important is being communicated to the apostles. Perhaps the apostles don't immediately take away the lesson from that scene, because at first they are amazed with Jesus.

"Who can this man be that even the seas and the storm obey him?" Even though this event opened their hearts more to believe in him, I believe Jesus wanted them to go even deeper. This first step towards wondering who Jesus is must be continually present in our journey of wonder and awe at Jesus. However, there's another thing that Jesus is stressing here: faith. Faith and acceptance.

There are two levels at which we can look at this event. The first is the level of the storm itself, which is prefigured in the Old Testament. One of the things that amazed the people of the Old Testament was that all the rivers flowed into the sea, and the sea never got full. It didn't keep creeping up on the shore and swallowing the land. They saw all the rain and the seas – but they didn't know about the transpiration cycle. So, they just saw more and more water going into the sea, and it never filled up. For them this was one of the marvels of God. The sea stayed where it was at the beach, and it never encroached the land. They knew it was God who was holding the sea at bay and making their life possible. That is why the first reading prefigures what is going to happen here with Jesus, and it helps us to enter into the reading more deeply. The first reading also helps us to understand that this miracle-parable of Jesus is not just about a storm and danger, but it is about the whole relationship between us and reality. Believe me, the fact that we do know about the transpiration cycle and we do know that the Earth is a sphere and that there's only so much water doesn't take anything away from the mystery of God. Even though we know that the wind can blow water up on the land a bit, and we've had some terrible tsunamis, we know it all goes back to its place. That knowledge doesn't take anything from our understanding of the mystery of God.

Today we celebrate Father's Day, and fatherhood is an extraordinary thing. Ultimately, I think the theme that underlies these readings today is the fatherhood of God. Why is Jesus asleep in the prow of the boat? What is he doing there? What about the question that the apostles ask him when they wake him up? They want to know if he even cares that they are going to sink. What is the answer to that question? How could Jesus be asleep in the prow of the boat? Here we catch a glimpse of Jesus' deeper understanding and the way he knows the world. We catch a glimpse of the way Jesus sees the world. In other words, we get to know the way the world really is. Ultimately what Jesus wants to tell the apostles is that everything truly is OK. You do not need to worry. Your life, your happiness, and the fulfillment of your life is not dependent on your ability to deal with things. If the apostles had been able to manage the storm, they wouldn't have woken up Jesus. If they had been able to make it over the next wave, and down into the next pit, and up over the next wave, and down into the next, they wouldn't have turned to Jesus. If the apostles thought they were in control and they had the situation in hand, they wouldn't have turned to Jesus. It is only when they realize that the situation is out of their hands that they turn to Jesus. Again, and again, and again, they turn to Jesus. Jesus is lying there asleep in the prow of the boat and we could say he is resting in the arms of his Father. The reason he is able to sleep in the prow of the boat during the storm is because he knows that he is in his Father's arms. And he knows that his Father is looking after him. He knows the truth behind the mystery that the people of Israel reflected on when the sea stays in its place. God is looking after us. And while the science in those days wasn't true, the reflection that they had was absolutely true. God is looking after us and protecting his people. God cares for us and we are in his hands. God is our Father in heaven, the One who looks out for us.

What are some of the characteristics of fatherhood? Well, one of the most essential is the ability to guide the young when they don't know what is for their good. Think about your own father. You are older now, like me. How many times did your father intervene to direct you toward your good in ways that at the moment you couldn't understand? In the same way, Jesus wants the apostles to be able to go and sleep in the boat, too. Ultimately we are all in that boat.

That boat isn't something very remote or distant; we are all in that boat at the point of sinking. We don't have the helm, and we are all at the point of going down and losing it. We are not in control. We know how tenuous this life of ours is. We know how the circumstances of life continually challenge us, and we can't even answer for one moment of it. So how do we live with that life of difficulties, struggles, problems, and all the things we have to deal with? Well, we need to call to the Lord now, in this moment. Because this is when everything is dramatic, just as it was for the apostles in the boat. We need to ask the Lord, as the apostles did, "Do you not care if I sink?" We need to turn to our Father and let him sustain us in our faith. Above all we need to beg that out of the experience of his Fatherhood we will grow in faith and trust.

There are many profound messages in this reading, but essentially, at its very heart, this reading are about the goodness of God. Therefore, these readings are about the ultimate positivity of everything in this reality of ours. The journey to the knowledge of that goodness is the journey of daily life. Knowledge of that goodness is found in living, day by day, in the circumstances that face us every day. Instead of thinking that the circumstances have to go, we need to call out to our Father. It is a little bit like Saint Thomas when he doubted Jesus and in that questioning he gave a great grace to the Church. The fathers of the Church often reflected upon Thomas. In his doubt, he gave us the opportunity to see Jesus revealing himself to the apostles and letting Thomas put his fingers in the wounds. Thomas himself also received this same reprimand as the apostles in the boat; he should have believed. But he did ask. There was another apostle there who didn't ask, who just left, and ended up committing suicide. Another one who doubted that Jesus would accomplish the happiness that he had promised. At least Thomas came back, and he asked.

In this Gospel the apostles do a similar thing for us. They show us that we need to call to the Lord always. We need to understand that peril is precisely in our inability to make things right. Probably the biggest danger that we have in our lives is that everything is OK. In some way we live in this steady state, in which tomorrow will be the same as today, and the next day the same, and the next day the same. We basically say, "What we've got now is OK." But my friends, what we have now is not OK. We're made for more. We're made for hunger. We're made for yearning. We're made for desire. For more, and more, and more.

Let us turn to Jesus in the prow of this boat of ours. And even while we fear to wake him, we need his word. The apostles needed his reassurance just as we need his reassurance. Let us turn to him and beg him for this gift of faith that he gives to those who ask. Let's ask for this gift as we celebrate this Holy Mass this morning.

I want to say a very brief word about the Pope's Encyclical, *Laudato Si*.'[14] I just want to say two words: read it. Please do not depend for your understanding and your consideration of the Pope's encyclicals on the many commentaries that will come to you from both sides of the political spectrum. Read it. Read it prayerfully and attentively. Remember who is writing the encyclical. It is our Holy Father the Pope, the one who guides the Church. And then I promise you that in the Fall, in August and September, we'll have opportunities to explore it, study it, and hear some people who can help us to engage with its content. We'll arrange those things. Right now, rather than give a whole load of opinions about it, and I know there are many opinions out there, let's read it. Maybe one or two have already read it, I don't know, but we should all have read it. We should all read it in these coming few weeks. It is already available online, but we will make sure it's available in the book shop just as soon as it becomes available. Read it. God bless you all.

---

[14] Pope Francis, "*Laudato Si*;'" (*Encyclical Letter*) Saint Peter's Square, May 24, 2015, http://www.vatican.va/content/francesco/en/encyclicals/documents/papa-francesco_20150524_enciclica-laudato-si.html.

August 3, 2014
Eighteenth Sunday in Ordinary Time

READINGS

First Reading: Isaiah 55:1-3
Second Reading: Romans 8:35, 37-39
Gospel Reading: Matthew 14:13-21

COLLECT

Draw near to your servants, O Lord, and answer their prayers with unceasing kindness, that, for those who glory in you as their Creator and guide, you may restore what you have created and keep safe what you have restored. Through our Lord Jesus Christ, your Son, who lives and reigns with you in the unity of the Holy Spirit, one God, for ever and ever.

The Economy of Grace

I don't know if people still collect stamps nowadays. When I was a kid I collected stamps. It was my first introduction to the laws of economics. I quickly came to realize the stamps that were very common were worth nothing, and the rarer a stamp was, the more it was worth. If there were only one or two of a very special stamp in existence, they were in the very top of the scale at prices beyond my imagining at the time. These are the laws of economics: when there is more, the value is less; when there is less, the value is more. We also know it from the economic cycles. A rumor of something that might interrupt the flow of oil is enough to make the prices at the pumps shoot up. The laws of economics seem to be inescapable.

Today's Gospel is interesting from that point of view. Here Jesus is talking about a life that works in almost exactly the opposite way to the laws of economics. That which is most precious, that which is most desirable, is free. We see it right here, in the first reading. It introduces the theme of today's Mass.

> All of you who are thirsty, come to the water. You who have no money, come, receive grain and eat. Come without pay and without cost, drink wine and milk. (Isaiah 55:1)

Can you image something that is free and doesn't increase in value because we all want it? Is there something that doesn't become more expensive because everyone's trying to get their hands on it? Do we live in a reality where something that is valued remains free – always? There are several places where Jesus talks about this reality. A few weeks ago, we heard:

> To him who has more, more will be given. And to him who has less, even what little he has will be taken away. (Matthew 13:12)

Try basing some social policy on that doctrine and you won't get very far. The dynamic of the life of the friendship with God is the reverse of the dynamic of this world. That which we want most earnestly is given to us freely, without any cost, and to everyone. It doesn't pit us, one against the other, because ultimately that's the law of the free market. If I gain, you lose; if you gain, I lose. It's a give and take. That is why the value goes up. Yes, you have that stamp. But if I want that stamp, I have to give you my car, my house, and everything else I possess and then I might be able to get that stamp from you. It pits us against one another, by its nature. And of course, then, we have many good laws that help to moderate competition, and indeed to turn it into the very productive force of our society.

The fact is, in an economic order, we are necessarily competitors. The world that Jesus introduces, however, is the world of grace, a world in which we are not competitors. We are truly for one another and support each other. Our gain is the other's gain. This only happens because what's available is without limit. In this sense, it does follow the economic order. The grace of God is available in an unimaginable quantity. There is more of it than we have ever dared to ask.

And this is the second great theme that we need to reflect on in today's readings. We haven't even begun to ask for the riches of God's grace. We haven't ever even begun to ask for the abundance, the bounty, and the fullness of life that God has to offer us. In order to understand this new order of grace that Jesus brings to the world, we have to consult our hearts. To know the order of the supernatural life Jesus offers, we have to consult our hearts because we need to be attached to that which is really worthwhile. And we need to use all the rest in function of that which is really worthwhile.

What does the Church say about the free market, the economy, and the laws of supply and demand? It does not say you should ignore them. The Church does not say you shouldn't compete. In fact, the Church supports free enterprise in society. It says indeed that it is a fundamental right of a person to be able to interact and engage in society and to produce and to benefit in the fruits of what one produces. However, that's not enough. Jesus said man does not live by bread alone. He didn't say bread isn't important. He said that there is something more important than the bread we eat. There is something more important than the money that we make. There is something more important than the stock that we hold or any other participation in the economic order. There is something more important.

That is exactly what Jesus is trying to do here with the people of Israel. The religion of Israel was not a religion of devotion. Instead, they had duty, laws, and cleanliness. Ritual cleanliness and ritual purity. Those were the things that they most treasured. You had to obey the law in every single detail that it entails. You had to be pure and could not let anything contaminate you. Just a little example of this: one law of the people of Israel says it is wrong to cook an animal in its mother's milk. So, you couldn't get a goat, and put some of the milk from the goat that you had milked the day before into the pot where you are boiling or stewing. That method was against the law. Nowadays, if you go to a truly Kosher household, they have two separate kitchens. One for the milks, and one for the meats. This way there is no chance that the law would ever be violated, because the ritual purity is the important thing. In a sense you could say that for the people who were following the law of Moses, everything caused them to look down and to pay attention to what they were doing. Did I walk too many steps on the Sabbath? It was all about what they did, what was done, and what took place. In this Gospel, Jesus is trying to tell them to lift their eyes. Look at a higher level and understand that there is something more, something greater, that your heart yearns to breathe. Saint Paul, of course, was a great witness to this because Saint Paul is the one who, more than anyone else, knew and tried living the law of Israel. Then he found life in Christ. All Paul's writings are practically a testimony of his discovery.

Back to today's theme. Jesus wants us to <u>not</u> be so involved in the economic order and all that has to do with the economic order, namely the world. That which we call an economic order, Saint John the Evangelist calls the world. He says you are in the world, but you are not of the world. By *the world* he means precisely that economic order that we are talking about. So, what does it mean to be in the world? We know that our jobs are important, and the advancement of our careers is important, especially at a certain stage in life when we are establishing ourselves. And we know that even our portfolios are important because we know we have to face our retirement. We know what it is to be in the world.

We know, for example, that if you want to send your kids to a Catholic school it costs money, and you have to put that money aside. We know what it is to be in the world. Jesus isn't telling us, "I'm taking you out of the world." Jesus leads us in the world. But then he also tells us that we are not of the world. You are in the world, but not of the world. What does it mean to not be of the world? It means precisely that we have our eyes fixed on him. In a prayer we've heard recently in the liturgy, our petition was that as we deal with the affairs of this world, let our hearts be fixed where our true joy can be found. Another prayer is, let our hearts be fixed on that which truly endures. So, the Church is always asking us to *raise our gaze*. Yes live in this world. Do the best you can for yourselves in this world, but lift your gaze. Understand that there's something you need that only God can give. He gives it in such abundance that it never runs out.

That's what this great miracle of the multiplication of the loaves is about. Jesus performs this miracle on at least two occasions. He works the same miracle in which he multiplies the food and gives it to the people. At first it seems that there is too little, and I can imagine someone sitting in the back saying, "There's only two fish and five loaves, and I'm way here in the back, what chance do I have of getting any?" You know those closest, the strongest, and the leaders are all going to get a little bit of fish, and the rest of us are going to go hungry. That is the way the world works. And that is probably what the people expected. Jesus simply says to just give out the food. Break it up and give it out. There is enough for everybody, and it's significant. The words of the Gospel say that everyone had their fill and was satisfied. Jesus gave something to everyone, and they were truly satisfied. When the people left, and the apostles collected the pieces, there were twelve baskets full. Why those twelve baskets? So they cousld waste food? No, rather so that we could learn that when we place our hearts where true joy can be found, when we seek that which endures forever, then there is plenty.

With Jesus, there is plenty, and the laws of the free market don't apply. My advantage isn't your disadvantage. Your advantage isn't my disadvantage. We are not always bidding against one another. That's the underlying dilemma of the free market; that we're always bidding. Everything is on auction, in a certain sense. That is not the way it is in the realm of grace: there is enough for everybody.

When we put that together with the fact that we have hungry souls, why haven't we found entirely what we are looking for? You know that song by U2, "I Still Haven't Found What I'm Looking For."[15] Maybe sometimes we need to sing that song ourselves. We need to sing it in our hearts when we are too caught up among the things of this world, or when we're

---

[15] U2, *The Joshua Tree,* Island Records, track 1, 1987, CD.

there worrying and worrying. How are we going to cover this, and how are we going to deal with that, and how are we going to solve this problem? In those situations, we can just think for a moment, "But I still haven't found what I'm looking for." Because it's not there. It's not on the desk or behind the computer screen. It is a gift, freely given by God, in totality and abundance. That is what I am looking for. All it takes is that rise of the gaze. That rise of the gaze that looks above the things of this world and understands the entire life of grace that God has given to us, which is illustrated to us so fully in the liturgy.

With this then in mind, let us turn now to our celebration of the Holy Mass, knowing that it is Jesus who is everything that we could possibly imagine. As we come up to the altar to receive the host, let us remember that in that host is all delight and all richness. Let us understand that the more we can find our satisfaction in Christ and in the Eucharist, the more we will be at peace. Then our engagement in the world, when we are in the world, allows us to use the world to our advantage; not to our egotistical advantage, but to the true advantage of our souls—which is, of course, the kingdom of heaven.

August 8, 2014
Memorial of Saint Dominic, Priest

READINGS

First Reading: Nahum 2:1, 3; 3:1-3, 6-7
Gospel Reading: Matthew 16:24-28

COLLECT

May Saint Dominic come to the help of your Church by his merits and teaching, O Lord, and may he, who was an outstanding preacher of your truth, be a devoted intercessor on our behalf. Through our Lord Jesus Christ, your Son, who lives and reigns with you in the unity of the Holy Spirit, one God, for ever and ever.

Saint Dominic's Proposal

Today we celebrate the feast of Saint Dominic, founder of the Dominicans and one of the great saints of the High Middle Ages. Saint Dominic started out as a diocesan priest. He lived at a time when the affairs of religion were also the affairs of State in the Christian world. He lived at a time where heresies were fought against not just by preaching, but also with arms because the very cohesion of the various kingdoms of Europe had at their heart the unity of faith. In Dominic's time, the heresy that was very popular was the Albigensian heresy, which the King of France sent his armies to suppress. However, Saint Dominic knew that the Christian proposal was not about coercion; it's about freedom. So, Saint Dominic, with his bishop, went out to preach and persuade. They understood that what comes to us from the very heart of the Christian message is always a proposal addressed to human freedom.

Therefore, while the king was sending his armies, Dominic and his bishop went on a mission of persuasion and preaching. It was on that mission of preaching that Dominic understood what a great task had to be done in this field, and he founded his order of preachers. At the very core of their work and life was mission: to go out among the people. Up until that moment, the consecrated life was a life of enclosure. You went into the monastery, you stayed in the monastery, and you lived your life in the monastery. But Saint Dominic understood that there was a need to go out into the highways and byways, into the villages and towns of the time and try to persuade people. Persuade simply means address arguments to their freedom.

Last week it was widely reported that Pope Francis said we shouldn't proselytize other people. Looking at Saint Dominic we can understand exactly what our Holy Father means by that. The proposal in Christianity is essentially an invitation to human freedom to come and follow, just as it was 2,000 years ago. There is a famous painting by Caravaggio of Jesus pointing his finger at the tax collector's office. He is pointing at Matthew and saying, "Come follow me." (Matthew 9:9) Matthew got up and followed him not because he was obliged or forced or cajoled to or because political pressure was brought on him to do it, but because he was struck and attracted by the invitation. Well, Saint Dominic founded his order precisely to address this attractive proposal to the people of his time and to win them back from the current heresies. His work was extremely fruitful. Even to this day, the Dominican order is one of the great and most vibrant and lively orders of the Church.

This was Saint Dominic's mission. At the time he seemed like an upstart or a revolutionary to some because he was breaking all the known models of his time. His monks—they were called friars—were not living their whole life in a monastery. Dominic's monks had at the center of their life a monastic life of prayer, but then they went out into the villages and towns and preached the Gospel. Slowly but surely both orders founded by Saint Dominic and his contemporary Saint Francis would establish a whole new way of living the consecrated life in the Church.

So, as we celebrate this Mass today, let us ask that we might respond to Christ the way Saint Dominic proposed—as an invitation. Let us ask that we might not be just living a tradition or living something that just kind of works on cruise control, but that we are engaged and within us there is a personal true free "Yes" to the Lord. Let us ask that our attachment to him might become ever more an engagement of our very selves and that any formality that exists may be conquered by a deep personal involvement to conversion. This is what Saint Dominic sought to do. One final point I'll make: it is always to the saints that you must look to see the truth of the Church in any generation. Reading the history of the Church without reading the lives of the saints is impossible.

August 9, 2014
Saturday of the Eighteenth Week in Ordinary Time

READINGS

First Reading: Hebrews 1:12-2:4
Gospel Reading: Matthew 17:14-20

COLLECT

God of our Fathers, who brought the Martyr Saint Teresa Benedicta of the Cross to know your crucified Son and to imitate him even until death, grant, through her intercession, that the whole human race may acknowledge Christ as its Savior and through him come to behold you for eternity. Who lives and reigns with you in the unity of the Holy Spirit, one God, for ever and ever.

Sowing the Invisible Seed of Baptism

It's not something that is immediately apparent. In our baptism, in the living faith to which we've been introduced, and which continues to live in us, we have a gift. Our baptism is a gift from God which as Jesus's parable here shows, isn't something immediately visible. It is not something that immediately reveals a power. Yet baptism is something that grows. It is something that truly transforms and makes us something completely new. That mustard seed was given to us is that tiny little thing that transforms us. When I do a baptism here at the Church it always strikes me how much the life of the world continues all around us. Out in the world, at the Flatirons mall and the streets and the roads of Broomfield and Denver, nobody is paying any attention to those of us gathered here in the church to perform a baptism. Nobody notices or pays attention, except those people who are here. Perhaps even we, who are here, are quite a bit distracted from what's going on. What is going on is precisely this sowing of that tiny seed that nobody is noticing but from which that sanctity grows. It is from that seed that the saints come. Think of any of the saints or the most familiar saints of our time. Think of Saint John Paul II. Think of Mother Teresa of Calcutta. Think of the saints that most of us remember in our lifetimes. It is precisely from the seed of baptism, from this tiny unnoticed seed that grows this great tree in which even the birds of the air can build their nests. So many find the possibility that they themselves also can live from that baptism which they have received in the lives of the saints. Let us ask, as we celebrate our Holy Mass then, for the gift of baptismal life.

Of course, we have baptismal life. Baptismal life isn't something that we have to acquire, but it is something to which we have to pay attention. It is something to which we have to give place. John Paul II used to always repeat that phrase, "Man, become what you are."[16] Let the baptized become what you are. Let us ask that we, the baptized, may become what we are. And that life sown in us may be allowed to flourish.

Jesus has another parable in which he speaks about the seed. We heard it a couple of Sundays ago at Mass, about the seed sown in the field. The seed sown on the good soil and the seed sown in all the different places. You know the parable. Jesus invites us to be that welcoming soil of the field that produces a rich harvest. In the opening prayer of the Mass this week we have that beautiful Collect in which it asks that we might live, even now, using the things that pass in order that we might ultimately possess the things that endure forever. In the midst of the small things of this world, may we hold in our hearts the things that endure forever. This is another way of explaining that Baptismal journey. The thing that endures forever is that life which was instilled in us, that was given to us, that was ignited in us at our baptism. That, my friends, is the life eternal that was given to us. That is the life that endures forever. Within that life is the true

---

[16] John Paul II, *Familaris Consortio: Of Christian Family in the Modern World* (Boston Pauline Books and Media, 1981), section #17

relationship with everything. Let us ask then, as we celebrate our Mass, that this Baptismal life in us may flourish.

August 11, 2019
Nineteenth Sunday in Ordinary Time

READINGS

First Reading: Wisdom 18:6-9
Second Reading: Hebrews 11:1-2, 8-19
Gospel Reading: Luke 12:32-48

COLLECT

Almighty ever-living God, whom, taught by the Holy Spirit, we dare to call our Father, bring, we pray, to perfection in our hearts the spirit of adoption as your sons and daughters, that we may merit to enter into the inheritance which you have promised. Through our Lord Jesus Christ, your Son, who lives and reigns with you in the unity of the Holy Spirit, one God, for ever and ever.

The Evidence in the Human Heart

Jesus introduces this discourse about faith with these words: "Do not be afraid any longer, little flock." This is the underlying theme of all of our readings today: fear is what's left when faith is taken away. Saint Thomas Aquinas says, "From nature springs the fear of death. From faith springs audacity."[17] By *audacity* he means the ability to truly live, to go forward and do things, to engage and live life to the full. Without audacity, fear is what dominates.

Faith is a gift that is given to us in many ways through the interventions God has accomplished on our behalf throughout the history of the world. Beginning with the call of Abraham, his great gesture of faith becomes the mark of the people of Israel. Faith instead of sacrifice. It is significant that God calls Abraham to sacrifice his son. This is the son in whom the fulfillment of God's promise to Abraham would seem to be entirely invested. It would seem that it is only through this son that the promise God made to Abraham can be realized: the promise that Abraham's children would be as numerous as the stars in the sky and grains of sand on the seashore. Therefore, this son is the hope of Abraham, and it is this son the Lord asks him to sacrifice. The ancient world held the belief that the greater the sacrifice you made, the more strongly you paid homage to God. That is why throughout

---

[17] See Thomas Aquinas, *Super Epistulam ad Corinthios Secundam*, commentary on 2 Corinthians 5:5-10, para. 165.

history, human sacrifice was always one of the extreme forms that the relationship with God could take, a deeply erroneous form. Here God takes the willingness of Abraham to offer his son and shows there is something even greater and more precious to God. What is truer in our relationship with God than sacrifice? Faith. The faith of Abraham who trusts in God is the origin of this Judeo-Christian faith we live today.

What does this faith do? Well, faith above all is often considered as a light; it illumines the world. Faith allows us to understand life beyond the borders of comprehension. It is impossible for us to put the pieces of life together in a way that is satisfactory to us as human beings without this gift of faith. The world in which we live today is a faithless world. It is a world that turns away from faith. Sometimes even we find this faithlessness nibbling away at our heels as though it is trying to grab us and pull us down into this world of unbelief. What then are some of the things that help us to believe? What are some of the things that support our belief? I would just like to spend a couple minutes pointing out a few of the sources that we can turn to in our faith.

The first great source of our faith is the very reality of being itself. The very existence of things is the first great evidence we can give in favor of our faith. While science is a beautiful adventure of exploration of the relationships that exist, the causes and effects that exist in reality, the being of reality itself is something that remains absolutely present. The being of things is something that cannot be eliminated. It is something that we can't get our minds around. It is not a phenomenon that can be explained by other phenomenon because it is the very place in which phenomena take place. It is the reality without which there would be no phenomenon.

So, let science engage in its beautiful adventure of exploring the phenomenon and its causes. We already know that the causes of the phenomenon are always other phenomenon. The eyes of science will always see phenomenon, or that which happens. That is a beautiful and great adventure. It runs toward a vanishing point where we are always looking for the phenomenon that underlies that last thing that we have understood and seen. And this is the journey of science. All of that is happening in a being, in a reality that already is. That my friends, is the first evidence of God's existence. The word *God* and the word *existence* are almost tautological. It is almost meaningless to say that God does not exist because it's a contradiction in terms. So, the first thing we can think about is that great evidence that is the being of reality.

The other great evidence for our faith is what I call the internal evidence. Being made for the relationship with God is deep within us. We are all familiar with that experience that Saint Augustine expresses: "Our hearts are made for you, O God, and will not rest until they rest in you."[18] The key to that statement is in that "will not rest" because it means there is something in our nature as humans that only finds its resolution in that relationship with God. This is precisely

[18] See Saint Augustine, *Confessions* (Lib 1,1-2,2.5,5: Corpus Scriptorum Ecclesiasticorum Latinorum 33, 1-5).

what Saint Augustine discovered. He was a man, who for many years of his life ran away from God. Finally, late in life, he discovers, "Late have I loved thee." Saint Augustine finally comes and makes his peace with God. Here he finds the answer to everything. This is evidence, my friends, this is evidence.

Scientists will observe the minutest phenomenon, the minutest anomaly in the phenomenon, and they will chase after that, they will pay attention to that, they will be vigilant and look at that, and they will discern a huge area of reality. The example I always give is those exo-planets that you so often see now in astronomy magazines. They are right there on the cover, these huge planets with their stripes. You can read about these planets that no one has ever seen through a telescope and no one has any idea what they look like. Where do they come from? How are they coming up with the descriptions? Is that picture on the cover of the magazine a pure invention? The fact is it is not an invention. It has been taken from the tiniest little inflection in a data stream coming from scientific instruments. By paying attention and being vigilant to that little blip inflection, studying and analyzing it, they are able to discern and eventually reconstruct the whole of the reality that is being revealed in that tiny little blip. This is the extraordinary thing about our time, but this is also why we should really be impatient with the world of unbelief. This world wants us to discard as meaningless and as having no informational content at all the evidence that abounds in the human heart. The world of unbelief wants us to ignore all of that human evidence showing the correspondence of our relationship with God to what we are made for. An example of this human evidence can be found in Saint Ignatius of Loyola.

Saint Ignatius, as you might know, received his vocation when he was convalescing after an injury. Saint Ignatius of Loyola was a man who loved adventure. He loved tales of errantry and great knights who went off and did great things. That was his passion; he loved to read these books. So, there he was convalescing in a castle and as he is beginning to get better, he asks, "Can you find me some books to read?" Of course, everyone knows what books he wants. He wants tales of errantry and the heroism of knights of old. His friends scour the castle from top to bottom but there isn't a single book like that. Maybe a little sheepishly they come along with a small stack of books, and they say, "Hey, Ignatius, we couldn't find any books about knights but here are some books about saints. Would you like to read these?" They put the books beside him and go away. Ignatius, perhaps a little bit reluctantly, picks up a book and starts reading.

He finds that these are great stories too. There is heroism on every single page. They delight him just as the stories of the knights delighted him. However, he does notice a difference. Ignatius notices that when he reads the tales of the knights, he is excited and drawn into the adventure, but when he puts aside the book and goes on with his day, he feels a weight. It is a weight of disappointment and dissatisfaction. On the other hand, when he reads the lives of the saints, he enjoys the book and it's a great story. When he puts the book aside, he notices something different happening inside his soul. He notices that now he is not disappointed, dissatisfied, impatient, and all of those things that relate to an absent good. In reality Ignatius is not a great knight, he is there with an injured leg not doing anything. Nothing that is happening in the knight's story is happening for him. However, when he finishes a book on the life of a saint, there is a deep joy that endures.

This is the thing that I want to point out to you. Ignatius pays attention to what is happening inside his soul. The scientist pays attention to the little inflection in the data stream and says, "What's going on here? This star, we're looking at it and it's just going hmmmm but it should be just absolutely steady. Stars are one of the most stable systems in the universe. It should be just stable, there's a blip there, let's have a look at this." The scientists take it seriously and we get our picture of this big exoplanet on the cover of our astronomy magazine. Saint Ignatius pays attention to that blip in his heart that is the difference in the outcome of an experience. The more he pays attention to that, the more he discovers that it's opening up a whole world to him. Ignatius is not discovering an exoplanet, but he is discovering the very life of union with God. Ignatius discovers the very thing for which he was made and that is the very key to his happiness. Building on this experience he is drawn into the relationship with God and he goes on to give his whole life to Christ. To a great degree Saint Ignatius of Loyola finds an answer to all of the problems brought up by the Reformation when he creates the Jesuit order. In those early centuries he sends out those Jesuits to spread the Gospel all over the world.

So, how does this evidence apply to us? It helps us to understand what Jesus means when he says "Be alert." It means exactly that we need to be attentive to who we are. Don't discard the evidence of your soul. Don't discard the evidence of your humanity. Don't try to live a life as if you did not exist because ultimately that is what the scientific mentality wants us to do. It is called the scientific mentality, but it is not scientific if it ignores the evidence that comes to us from our humanity.

Two great pillars that can sustain and support our faith. There is the first pillar of the natural order, which you can meditate on in many, many ways. I gave you the primary example of being. Then there is the second pillar, the interior life. In this life exists the map of our humanity, the identity of our humanity, and the evidence that emerges in our humanity of God. Faith is a gift and therefore it must always be asked for and prayed for. We must ask for faith. Few prayers are as fruitful in life as the prayer for faith. We know Saint Thomas' famous prayer: "Lord I believe. Help my unbelief." This is a great and beautiful prayer because it acknowledges the world of unbelief that nibbles at our heels, a world in which everyone thinks that belief is now out of date, out of fashion, overcome, and bypassed. It is still a prayer of faith: Lord, I believe; help my unbelief. Help me to grow in faith. We need to grow in faith. There is no one here who cannot grow in faith. All of us need to grow in faith. From faith grows hope: from faith comes trust, and from trust comes hope. From hope comes the adventure of life lived to the full.

Let us ask for an increase in faith as we celebrate this Mass. Let us ask as the Church puts before us in the readings this great gift of faith. Let us ask that we might be vigilant, and in our vigilance we might recognize his presence in the many signs and imprints of his presence in the world. Let us pray that we, like Ignatius, may allow our lives to be drawn into a totalizing relationship with him, because that is what he desires from each of us. Let us ask for these graces for one another.

August 15, 2016
Solemnity of the Assumption of the Blessed Virgin Mary – Vigil Mass

READINGS

First Reading: 1 Chronicles 15:3-4, 15-16; 16:1-2
Second Reading: 1 Corinthians 15:54B-57
Gospel Reading: Luke 11:27-28

COLLECT

Almighty ever-living God, who assumed the Immaculate Virgin Mary, the Mother of your Son, body and soul into heavenly glory, grant we pray, that, always attentive to the things that are above, we may merit to be sharers of her glory. Through our Lord Jesus Christ, your Son, who lives and reigns with you in the unity of the Holy Spirit, one God, for ever and ever.

A Simple Prayer to Mary

Jesus says in reply to a woman who was praising his mother, "Rather, blessed are the people who hear the word of God and observe it." Many people interpret this as a put-down to our Blessed Mother Mary. Sometimes even our Protestant brothers and sisters use this text to prove that we shouldn't honor Mary the way we do. In actual fact, what we are showing by that concern is just how, in today's culture, we are constantly measuring the emotional temperature of everything. That is not the way they were in the days of Jesus. They were very, very objective people. We, however, feed so directly into what we think is the emotional content that we imagine Mary feeling really offended and put down when in actual fact Mary was more honored by Jesus' answer than by the woman who cried out. The woman in the crowd who was praising Mary was giving her a biological glory. The woman was praising Mary as worthy and wonderful because she gave birth to this wonderful man that we have here in front of us. Jesus instead points out the very way in which Mary's greatness is most exalted, and that is by her hearing God and obeying his will. Mary is an example for everyone and Jesus points to the example. Mary heard the word of God and observed it.

This Mary, who pondered all things in her heart, was not somebody who was looking for emotional affirmation. She was rock solid in her absolute conviction that she was a loved one of God whom God had looked upon in her lowliness. Tomorrow morning the readings on this great feast day includes the Magnificat, which is exactly Mary's awareness of who she was and where her greatness comes from. Mary is more glorified by the fact that Jesus points at the obedience to the will of God as a thing that truly constitutes greatness. Mary is the prime example, the supreme example of that faithfulness. In Mary's "Yes" given to the angel, and to God, who sent the angel to her, is an affirmation of everything that God intended and wanted to do.

There are many titles for Mary. One of them is the New Eve because she undid what Eve did. Adam and Eve chose disobedience, but Mary chose obedience. It was God's choice to hinge the reversal of the tragedy of Adam and Eve at the very foundations of humanity on Mary's response. Mary responded in a moment of freedom in which she answered with her assent to the divine plan. Therefore, Mary is creating for us a whole new possibility in this human condition of ours, even though we do recognize this world as a valley of tears. We know that the tears are not what dominates. The love of God is what has triumphed—the love that was revealed in Jesus on the cross and triumphant in his resurrection. This is the sort of world that through Mary's "Yes" we came to inherit. For you and I who come 2,000 years later, Mary is the model of everything.

The particular event we celebrate today is that Mary concluded her earthly life and was assumed body and soul into heaven. Heaven for us is a little bit difficult to fathom, because it seems so unreal. It seems like a nice wish. But the faith of the Church from the very beginning is rock solid about heaven, eternal life, and the resurrection of our bodies.

It is certainly true that we can't imagine heaven. We can't get a picture of heaven. Jesus didn't choose to give us an image or to help us to understand how heaven works. We who send rockets to the outer planets now, and to moons and comets and all sorts of things, find it hard to imagine what heaven could be, where it might be, what it might look like, or what the experience of being there might be. All of that is true; it is hard to imagine. Never allow that inability to create a doubt about the truth. Our truth is not based on an image of what heaven would be like, but on the fact that God revealed to us his desire that where he is, we might also be. And when Jesus spoke about heaven, he used the most practical images he could. "There are many dwelling places in my Father's house." (John 14:2) He constantly gave us a physical language for this reality of heaven. As an article of faith, at the very core of our faith, we believe that we who have been baptized in Christ will rise again. We who do not reject that baptism, but live our baptismal life, and persevere until the end in baptismal life, believe that we will live forever with him in a place called heaven. The fact that we cannot imagine it has nothing to do with its truth and reality.

In fact, Mary ascended body and soul into heaven; she's already there. You can turn to her and say a little prayer:

> Mary, you're already there. You're where I want to go. You are already enjoying the ultimate goal of my existence, which is union with God in the kingdom of heaven. Help me to get there too. Help me to arrive where you already are.

This is a very simple and humble prayer. It is a very effective prayer, too.

Another thing that our theology says about Mary is that she is the pattern of the fullness of the human condition. A human being who lives life to the full will become ever more like Mary in the essentials: in the type of soul, the type of heart, the type of attitude with which she lived her life. We, too, are invited to identify with Mary. Mary above all is the most perfect image of the human condition realized by one of us mortal creatures. We can turn to her and ask her for strength, support, and intercession. In Mary we can find all of these things that help us to live this human condition of ours.

There is a period, perhaps when one is young, when one can think in this world, “This deal is OK.” But the more you look at this world the more you realize that 90 years is simply not acceptable for the human soul. Even 150 years is not acceptable to the human soul. And rightly, every fiber of our human soul cries out and says “No” to death. Death is not alright. Jesus came precisely to win a victory over death. Mary illustrates the fullness of Jesus’ victory over death for us by her assumption into heaven. That victory over death that Jesus won, that we see realized in Mary, is the victory to which each one of us is called, every bit as much as Mary.

As we celebrate Mary’s assumption into heaven, let us make that simple prayer our own. Let us pray that she might help us to get there ourselves in fullness when we’ve completed the years he gives us. Let us ask for this grace.

August 23, 2017
Wednesday of the Twentieth Week in Ordinary Time

READINGS

First Reading: Judges 9:6-15
Gospel Reading: Matthew 20:1-16

COLLECT

O God, you set Saint Rose of Lima on fire with your love, so that, secluded from the world in the austerity of a life of penance, she might give herself to you alone; grant, we pray, that through her intercession, we may tread the paths of life on earth and drink at the stream of your delights in heaven. Through our Lord Jesus Christ, your Son, who lives and reigns with you in the unity of the Holy Spirit, one God, for ever and ever.

Going to the Marketplace

Do you ever wonder about those people who were waiting in the marketplace at 5 o'clock in the afternoon? What were they doing when Jesus came out in the morning, and when he came out midday? What about the ones he found still waiting in the marketplace? Were they taking a nap? Were they having a lie on? What were they doing? The fact is that they weren't there at the first hour. They weren't there at the second hour. But they were there at the third hour. At the third hour the Lord came out to meet them and invite them into his harvest. Through that invitation, Jesus calls us to experience the fullness of life. That's what this parable of Jesus is about.

What does it mean, then, to be in the marketplace? What is the significance in this parable that there are people in the marketplace, in the sun, waiting for a job? I think it means to take the issue of life seriously. It means to no longer just live on the surface of life but begin to turn around and look for the meaning, the purpose, and to seek to understand what life is about. It means Jesus wants us to really engage with this life and to live it, truly, correctly, and rightly.

What are we arriving at? Are we even in the marketplace yet, or do we find ourselves still disengaged? Do we find ourselves still just hanging out? Have we truly come to the marketplace to look for a job? Have we come to the Lord looking for an involvement in his great plan for our lives? I think the first and most important message that we can learn from this parable is that there is a way in which we can make ourselves impervious to God's grace. That happens through self-satisfaction. It happens through being satisfied with the little things and with what we've got. Maybe when we are young and strong, we can be satisfied with our possessions and our relationships and say, "I have enough." As years go by, slowly but surely we know that there is something bigger looming on the horizon. Perhaps when we first notice it, we still turn our head down when we look at this world. As years go by, we find ourselves having to look up and ask ourselves, what is this all about? What is it all for, what does it mean, this human life of ours? What am I here to do? What is the purpose of this existence? Perhaps it is only when that great presence on the horizon is looming large that I finally go out to the marketplace and wait for an encounter with the Lord. Perhaps by the grace of God we get out there earlier. But I think few of us are there the first hour. Maybe there are more of us out there the second hour, and there are probably an awful lot of us there the third hour. We have tried everything else first, all the other solutions. Finally, toward the end of the day we come to our Lord to help find the path, to help find the way. This is the first lesson.

The second lesson is this: that the Lord invites us. He is waiting for us whenever we come. And when we come, he invites us into his vineyard. What is that vineyard to which he invites us? That could be nothing but the normal life of the Church, the normal Christian life. I don't know if you understand just how great a treasure we have in the long traditional Catholic life. We go to Mass on Sundays, we say our prayers in the morning and the evening, and if we sin we go to confession before we go to communion. If we don't have any mortal sins, we go to confession from time to time to receive God's healing graces anyway. We say our prayers and receive our sacraments. We live the Catholic life. That's the labor of the vineyard. Jesus didn't set up something difficult for us. If he had set up some extraordinarily difficult task, we could complain, but we have nothing to complain about. He gave us a beautiful, simple journey that is punctuated more than anything else by our presence here around the altar on Sunday. This is the biggest single part of the invitation that Jesus makes to us to come to his vineyard; that we gather here, every Sunday, around the altar to celebrate the great feast of his life. The Mass that takes place on the altar is called *agape*. *Agape* is the Greek word for divine love, for the love of God. That is the feast given to us from this altar. The wages Jesus gives to us for this labor in his vineyard are not just any wages, but the gift of his very self. This introduces us to the second great theme in today's readings: God always exceeds our expectations.

We have come at the third hour, and spiritually we can all consider ourselves as having come at the third hour. In fact, it is the most proper place for us to put ourselves: at that third hour. Why do I say this? Maybe you have been a cradle Catholic, and you've never stopped going to Mass all your life. Praise the Lord if that's what happened; that's a blessed thing. But there is still an aspect under which we haven't come to the Lord truly in poverty of spirit. So, if it's the third hour, and we come in, he fills us, he gives us the fullness of life. What did he do for each of the wage earners, the ones who came in the morning, midday, and afternoon? To each one he gave a full day's wage. And the full wage doesn't represent something small, it represents fullness. Completeness. God gives us everything, my friends. He truly does give us everything. But he gives us everything that we don't expect. Which would you prefer? Would you prefer to find an extra $100,000 in your bank account, or would you prefer to receive the gift of God's love. You see, that's what it comes down to. If we find this religion doesn't really touch our lives, it is because we don't perceive really and truly its value. The $100,000 extra in our account, we perceive that right away. Immediately possibilities, ramifications come to mind, and we are delighted. But when we receive this extraordinary gift of love from God, we tend not to notice or even see it. My friends, we can only see it if we are really out there in the marketplace looking for a job. If we don't see that gift of God that is love, as something of value, then it means we are really still in bed, and Jesus is out there in the marketplace looking for workers. We are simply not there. To come to the marketplace means to be truly poor in spirit. And to be poor in spirit means to have a hungry heart full of desire for something more. Man does not live by bread alone, neither does woman live by bread alone. None of us lives by bread alone. Jesus told us that. Here bread represents the material things, the new cars, the new houses, the jewelry, the clothes, the electronic gadgets, the cruises and vacations to exotic parts of the world, all of those things are part of the bread. What Jesus said is all of those things, wonderful and all though they are, simply are not enough. In the end they leave you disappointed. "Is this all there is?"

I don't know if any of you have come to that point in your life yet where you look around at all the abundance of things, and you say, "Is this really all there is?" I remember a friend of mine who used to spend all of his income on his stereo system. He had his whole wall plastered with all the components and various things. He had a beautiful leather chair on front of it, with all the controls for his stereo built into the hand rest. One day when I was visiting, and he was showing me all his stuff, he said, "Michael, you know, sometimes I sit here and scream, 'Make me happy! Make me happy! You've got all my income. You've got everything I've earned these last twenty years, now make me happy.' That's the beginning of poverty of spirit. We have to discover in our own hearts the truth that man does not live by bread alone. (Matthew 4:4) We have to discover in our own hearts the need for something greater. Because when we go to that marketplace looking for something greater, we will realize the value of the preciousness of the gift of God's life. Once we get that, we will never willingly leave him. If we get lost, we'll come right back, just as quickly as we possibly can.

My friends, let us ask that at the very least we may go out into the marketplace and look for a job. Let us look for an involvement with the real substance of life. Let us ask for that, because I know if we go out there to that marketplace looking for a job, the Lord will invite us in. He will allow us to work in his vineyard and will give us a reward that far exceeds anything we expected. Let us ask for these graces for ourselves and for one another.

October 20, 2016
Thursday of the Twenty-ninth Week in Ordinary Time

READINGS

First Reading: Ephesians 3:14-21
Gospel Reading: Luke 12:49-53

COLLECT

May the Priest Saint Paul, whose only love was the Cross, obtain for us your grace, O Lord, so that, urged on more strongly by his example, we may each embrace our own cross with courage. Through our Lord Jesus Christ, your Son, who lives and reigns with you in the unity of the Holy Spirit, one God, for ever and ever.

An Original Fire

This Gospel is somber. But we must remember that in this Gospel, Jesus is the first one who is going to enter this crucible of opposition that love evokes in this world. That's the fire that Jesus is bringing into the world, the fire of real, true, human love; the love of the human heart, when it encounters and finds that for which it was made, and when it is united with that for which it was made. At this moment there appears in the world a protagonist. A person who is truly a protagonist is a main character who is not determined by the ebb and flow of things that come and go. A person who has an original source of life in that loving relationship with God is a protagonist. That is what the true adult, the true Christian is. That is what the saint is. A saint is a person whose life is founded on that loving relationship with the God of love. That person acts in the world, not as a responder, not as somebody who responds to what's going on, but as a person who is with the Creator. A responder is someone who takes positions here and there depending on their likes and dislikes. A saint is a person who has an ultimate sympathy for all of being, for all of reality. Therefore, a saint is a person who enters into all of the situations of life with an original position, whether it be the office, family, or various social groups of all types. That position is the creative, forceful fire of the divine love. But my friends, that position is not welcomed in this world. Jesus himself was not welcomed, and he was the first to show us perfect love, because in Jesus love is total and perfect. There isn't a single gesture made by Jesus that isn't an expression of love. There isn't a single word of Jesus that isn't an expression of love. There isn't a single gaze of Jesus that isn't a perfect expression of love. There isn't a single teaching that isn't a teaching of perfect love.

Instead of finding the welcome of humanity for that thing which humanity is made for and longs for, Jesus finds precisely this sword, which he says he comes to bring to the world. He doesn't come to bring to the world the sword because he wants the destruction of the world, he does it because the world does not want its own good. The world does not want this love for which it is made. This is also inevitably the path of the Church and the saints in the world. The saint in the world doesn't automatically receive admiration for that journey to holiness that sainthood requires. Rather, the saint's life provokes opposition. Look at Saint Francis who was practically driven out of his own order in his own lifetime. There are so many examples of the way saints don't provoke universal accord and acceptance.

As we celebrate the Holy Mass today, and as we stand in front of this teaching, let us ask the Lord for this original fire. Let us ask the Lord that we might truly admit the fire into our lives. Here is the thing about the fire: it embraces and consumes the persecution. It really does consume the persecution. It is a good swap to win the love of God and to lose, in some degree, the esteem, respect, and honor in this world. It's a good exchange, even as one is living it. The saints and even the martyrs didn't hanker after a more secure place in society when they went to their martyrdom. They were full of fire that consumed all of the evil they had to face and brought the redemptive participation in the very sacrifice of Christ. We don't need to ask for persecutions. Let the Lord worry about them. What we need to do is ask for the fire. Ask for this fire that Jesus yearns might come to the earth. The reason the fire is not coming to the earth rapidly is because we are wet wood. We are slow to take flame. Jesus is there all the time trying to kindle the fire, but the fire never gets going. Let us ask that the fire may get going in our lives.

October 22, 2017
Twenty-ninth Sunday in Ordinary Time

READINGS

First Reading: Isaiah 45:1, 4-6
Second Reading: 1 Thessalonians 1:1-5B
Gospel Reading: Matthew 22:15-21

COLLECT

Almighty ever-living God,
grant that we may always conform our will to yours and serve your majesty in sincerity of heart.
Through our Lord Jesus Christ, your Son,
who lives and reigns with you in the unity of the Holy Spirit,
one God, for ever and ever.

Give to God What Is God's

In the first reading we heard, "I am the Lord, there is no other. There is no God besides me." Then in the responsorial psalm, "We give glory and honor to God." And we repeat, "That there is no God but the Lord, that God is truly Lord of all." And then in the Gospel, we read "Render unto Caesar what is Caesar's, and unto God what is God's."

The Pharisees had decided that they needed to deal with Jesus. Their first reaction was to deal with him politically. Eventually they would use stronger means, but right now they want to do it politically. To compromise Jesus they need to force him into some politically incorrect speech. They needed to be able to look at him with opprobrium and discard him as somebody who does not have the right political opinions. Therefore, they think through this little test they give to Jesus. It is not just something devised in the spur of the moment; it's the outcome of a caucusing with the Herodians to find something that is really going to force Jesus to be on the wrong side. The conspirators need something that is going to make Jesus, whichever way he goes, say something that will cause scandal and horror to be reported on the front pages of the newspapers the next day. I know that is anachronistic, but that's the logic that's going on here. Let's get Jesus into a place where we can ridicule him.

This would work if Jesus had been a political operative. However, because what generates and moves Jesus is not political interests, but rather truth, their tactic does not work.

All Jesus has to do is go back to the truth of the question. When speaking the truth of the question, the solution becomes obvious and simple. "Render unto Caesar what is Caesar's, and unto God what is God's."

This is an important thing to understand. Let's start with God. What is his part? As the first two readings showed us very clearly, God's part is everything. It truly is everything. There's nothing that is not God's part. All is of God. Show me something you have that wasn't given to you, as Father Giussani used to say when he was trying to help us to understand our radical dependence on God. Show me something now, anything, that you have that was not given to you. Show me what you brought into this world as your right. Nothing. God is all in all. God is the owner of all, the maker of all, the arbitrator of all, and in the truest sense, everything belongs to God. So, what's God's part? It's not a part – it's everything. That is the first thing that has to be clear.

What does Jesus mean by "Render unto Caesar what is Caesar's"? What he means to do is to identify something happening there that the Catholic tradition has picked up right from the very beginning. You find already in the Old Testament this idea that God gave the world to men. He gave the world to us human beings as stewards of the created world. We are stewards of creation. As such, God established a worldly order that is legitimate. Tell me where Jesus said in the Gospel to overthrow the Emperor? He never said that. He accepted the order entirely and completely, and he lived entirely and completely within that order that was established by the autonomy of man. Jesus does not question the gift of being allowed by God to establish what we might today call, an economic order. What Jesus is saying is that we can give that to Caesar. Let Caesar have what God already gave him. Let Caesar have what is entrusted to him and be the steward over those things that God gave him. However, like everyone else, Caesar has to remember that the day will come when he will see God face to face and answer for that stewardship.

Taking that coin and looking at the head of Caesar on the coin and saying "Render unto Caesar what is Caesar's," Jesus is entrusting; he is recognizing the stewardship that God has given to Caesar, and analogously to each one of us for that part of the world that the Lord has entrusted to our care. It may be our homes and our families, it may be the companies for which we work, or the departments for which we are the managers; there are so many things. Certainly, our income, and our bank accounts, and our vote. I'm going to come to that thing about the vote now in a few moments, because that is really one of the things over which we have stewardship. As a community, in this democratic form of government, we have stewardship over those who run the country as well.

God says let them have theirs. Everything belongs to God and he entrusts the administration of the created order to man as stewardship. But then Jesus says that you must render unto God what is God's. What is God's? Well of course everything. But what is God's in a very special way is us. What belongs to God is our humanity, our personhood, and our freedom. To use a Father Giussani expression again, the thing we mean when we say "I." "I want this," or "I vote for this," or "I give you this." That is the thing that most preciously is God's. If you read through the Gospel, you'll find the thing that Jesus takes most seriously is his encounter with the "I," the person. His encounter with the person and the response of that person to that encounter is the thing that most profoundly and deeply interests Jesus.

So it is here today. It is us on front of God. What we say in the depths of our heart, and the depths of our personhood, to God is what God is most interested in. That is, of all God's things, and everything is his, the thing that he treasures most is what he sent his Son into the world for. The object of the salvation Jesus brings is us. It's my personhood. If we truly live the journey of our own personhood, then the social order and the created order will be looked after as well. We need to go and live in society as free people. We need to live as people who are truly endowed with freedom that was created by God. This is one of the strategies that the Pharisees and Herodians come up with. They think, if Jesus says, "Yes, yes pay the taxes," then he's giving in and renouncing the very strong sense that the people of Israel had as being God's people. God's chosen people are slaves to no one, right? (John 8:33) "We are the sons of Abraham and we have never been a slave to anyone," one of the Pharisees one day protested to Jesus. They have this very strong sense of their personhood. We should have that sense, too. We should have that sense of our freedom, and it should be a very strong sense.

However, that freedom is lived out only in giving to God what is God's. When we fail to give to God what is God's, we abuse our freedom and we ultimately destroy it. It's not that we use it frivolously, it is that we ultimately destroy it. It is like telling someone in a prison cell, "You can go anywhere you want, you are free to go." What he does, though, is go back into the prison cell. Imagine one of those confessions in the prison cell, and I say to you, "You can go anywhere you want; you can go home to your family, you can do anything you want," and you go back into the prison cell and you lock door and you say "This is where I want to be." When we pursue freedom without giving to God what is God's, that's what we do; we destroy the very gift of freedom that we have.

I always think it's interesting that we come up with this reading as election time rolls around. We are free, my friends, we are free, and our vote really does count. It counts an awful lot. Our vote must be made in that sense, that while we know that God has entrusted the worldly order to us as stewards, a very important part of that stewardship is the way we vote. We must vote as a people who truly give to God what is God's.

We could work this out across the whole political spectrum if we wanted, but since this pro-life month, I'll just take the issue of life as an example. This issue makes it very clear how to render unto God what is God's. One of the criteria by which we must vote: God creates the human person. Our pro-life position is based on a simple fact that the person belongs to God. We believe that every person belongs to God. We have no right to violate that person at any point from their first creation to the end of their natural life. That belongs to

God. The person belongs to God, and we must honor the person. We can't discard that. If we do, then we fail to give to God what is God's and thereby fail in our stewardship. We fail to treasure what God has given. The pro-life position isn't an anti-position. It isn't a position against anyone or anything. It's a position for. It is for God's gift of life. We have to keep that in mind. We can't engage in the stewardship of the created world without bearing that in mind. This is why we talk about the need to vote for what is truly good. It's incumbent on everyone to use our vote for that which is good and not for that which is evil. We use our vote to serve the common good and participate in genuine stewardship of the world that God has given us. We are stewards of that which God has entrusted to our care.

We have to say that we can truly do what Jesus tells us to do here. We can give to God what is God's, and give to Caesar what is Caesar's. This doesn't pull us in two different directions. It doesn't make us a divided person. It comes together in one simple thing. Let us ask as we live out this season of the year, that we might give to God what is God's, and give to Caesar what is Caesar's. Let us ask for this grace for ourselves and for one another.

November 17, 2016
Memorial of Saint Elizabeth of Hungary, Religious

READINGS

First Reading: Revelation 5:1-10
Gospel Reading: Luke 19:41-44

COLLECT

O God, by whose gift Saint Elizabeth of Hungary recognized and revered Christ in the poor, grant, through her intercession, that we may serve with unfailing charity the needy and those afflicted. Through our Lord Jesus Christ, your Son, who lives and reigns with you in the unity of the Holy Spirit, one God, for ever and ever.

Creatures with Open Eyes

I would like to take a moment today to talk about those creatures from the Book of Revelation whom we just read about. The Book of Revelation is a very particular literary form. It's a form in which so many teachings are communicated through striking images. We can't make anything cute of this. When we start to think of a lamb, we think of something cute, furry and cuddly, but all of a sudden there are swords coming out of its mouth and there are eyes all over its body, and any idea that it is something cute and sentimental is immediately taken away. We have to understand that there is something very clear and very strong being communicated here. For example, just take all those eyes. You try to imagine those creatures and all of a sudden, they are covered in eyes. You and I know that one of the things said about Christians today is that they have their eyes closed; that they don't look, that they don't know. It is also said that we are afraid of science and knowledge. In this Gospel scene we have creatures covered in eyes that see everything. Eyes inside and eyes outside that are really truly aware of everything. These creatures come and worship before God himself.

We can see in this example the simple fact that our worship of God is not some opium of the people that Marx talked about, and it is not some closing of the eyes or averting of the human gaze from what's really within us and outside us.

Rather, we see in this example an awareness of everything. The one who is truly willing to look at everything and not to exclude anything from perception will truly and ultimately become a worshipper of God. The one who is truly courageous will recognize that God is the one to whom all worship, honor, and glory is due. The eyes of that person see. We don't have to close our eyes in order to have faith, we need to open our eyes to everything. For example, it's been reported recently that Pope Francis spoke about evolution and said that God is not a magician. If you know about this, then you know that this has been a Catholic tradition for a very, very long time. You even find it already in the fathers of the Church. You needn't be scandalized by the Galileo story that everyone throws in our face. If you study the Galileo story, you will discover that at the very core of the story is not some refusal to look at the evidence of nature but rather a presumption to draw theological and scriptural conclusions from the evidence of nature.

The point is that we are not afraid to keep our eyes open. Our worship of the Lord is never confounded by what we see. What we see through the eyes of science, provided it is a noble, open, and true science that innocently seeks the truth, is that we need never be afraid of the science about the universe, biology, or any other aspect of this created world in which we find ourselves. Pope Benedict himself spoke at a conference on evolution, which became a book that I would recommend to you.[19] It is a short book, but he deals adequately with the long-standing Catholic position about the observation and the awareness of the natural world. So, the one who is more covered with eyes is the one who will more truly worship and recognize the almighty power of God and recognize that to him is due all worship and honor.

As we celebrate Mass today, let us ask that we might have the true confidence of faith. The trouble with closing your eyes in order to believe is that you end up not really believing at all. Rather you end up knowing deep, deep down inside that you've fooled yourself. There's no need to close the eyes. All of the discoveries of science only deepen our sense of wonder and mystery at the created order and our sense of its extraordinary origin and being. So, I think we can leave this thought here for today. We can truly open our eyes with loyal hearts and clear thought. It will always become clear to us that the more we truly see, the more we perceive the truth. Ultimately, the truth is expressed beautifully and synthetically in the phrase we just read: "To him the honor and glory is due forever and ever, holy, holy, holy, mighty God."

We could also then develop a little line of thought about the internal eyes. What do we see with those internal eyes? What do we discover with those internal eyes? Because those internal eyes ultimately perceive an infinite need, an infinite abyss, and an infinite capacity in the human soul that needs

---

[19] S.D.S. Stephan Horn, ed., *Creation and Evolution: A Conference with Pope Benedict XVI in Castel Gandolfo* (San Francisco, CA: Ignatius Press, 2008).

fulfillment—a need that can only find fulfilment in God. As Saint Augustine says, "Our hearts are made for you, O God, and cannot find rest until they find that rest in you."[20] Both our external eyes, and our internal eyes will all ultimately give witness to our creature-li-ness, to our belonging to God, and to our recognition of his Son and Lord who has come into the world.

---

20 See Saint Augustine; *Confessions* (Lib 1,1-2,2.5,5: Corpus Scriptorum Ecclesiasticorum Latinorum 33, 1-5)

November 7, 2016
Monday of the Thirty-second Week in Ordinary Time

READINGS

First Reading: Titus 1:1-9
Gospel Reading: Luke 17:1-6

COLLECT

Almighty and merciful God,
graciously keep from us all adversity, so that, unhindered in mind and body alike, we may pursue in freedom of heart the things that are yours. Through our Lord Jesus Christ, your Son, who lives and reigns with you in the unity of the Holy Spirit, one God, for ever and ever.

The Servant's Voice

The Pope receives a title on the day of what used to be called his coronation. In more recent years, popes have moved away from that language seeking to disavow a claim to worldly power. Pope Benedict has even gone so far as to remove the three crowns from the Papal emblem. At that elevation to the chair of Peter, one of the titles that the Pope is given is the Servant of the Servants of God.

It's very important we understand that the Church is at the service of everyone. The Church is at our service. The Church is set up just like Christ came into the world "For us men, and for our salvation" as we say in the Profession of Faith. The Church exists for us. It is our servant. However, the Church cannot serve us by simply ministering to our wants, likes, and feelings. The Church has to serve us as the reminder and sign of God's presence among us. It is only in gathering around that presence on the altar that we are saved. It is only in gathering around that presence that we are truly served. For example, if the Church, with its answer, does what all the modern voices call out to the Church to do, that is to get with the times, then the Church would betray us. The Church wouldn't serve us. Only by being that voice that calls us to live not for the immediate, but for the truth, can the Church save us. To serve us the Church must remind us to live not on the surface, but for what is deepest and truest in all of being.

One of the central moments in the Mass is the prayer that comes immediately before the readings called the Collect.

The Collect is the prayer that expresses what the Church is asking for as she is united in the liturgy: in Christ as the head of this Church, and in this particular Mass. All this week we have been saying this prayer, which is very beautiful:

> O God, who have prepared for those who love you
> good things which no eye has seen.[21]

That's the thing, no eye has seen. We immediately go for what the eye sees on the surface. It glitters, it's nice, it's attractive, I'll take it. But the truest and deepest goods are goods that no eye has seen.

> Fill our hearts, we pray, with the warmth
> of your love. So that, loving you in all things, and above all things we may attain your promises, which surpass every human desire.

What does "Loving you in all things, and above all things" mean? We already know what above all things means, that we should love God above everything else. God should be our highest good. He's not God if he's not our highest good. Whenever we remember God, but we don't hold God as the highest good, we would immediately call it idolatry. Anything that we term God in our life that isn't our highest good, is not God. Any God that fits in to our scheme of things and is an element in our life, that's not God. God cannot be turned into that, and it's not God. The only God who is a true God is the

---

[21] See t*he English Translation of Collects from The Roman Missal*, International Commission on English in the Liturgy Corporation, 2010, Twenty-First Sunday in Ordinary Time.

God who is above all and is the criteria of all. God is above all things.

"In all things." What does loving God in all things mean? It means precisely that everything is loved in him in the light of that truth. Therefore, if I cooperate with you in misdirecting you or distracting you or emphasizing and amplifying the temptations and allures of this world, if I participate with you in any of those things, then I'm not loving you. I'm not loving God in you, and the only way I can truly love you is loving you in God.

So loving God in all things and above all things, we may attain his promises. You know every time we say the *Angelus* or the *Hail, Holy Queen*, we have that beautiful doxology and we should always pause for a moment when we say it. When we say, "Pray for us O Holy Mother of God, that we may be made worthy of the promises of Christ," we should always pause. We should think about that little phrase, "The promises of Christ." We should be aware of those promises, because, as this prayer goes on to say, they surpass every human desire. In other words, that's our true interest.

Now to go back to the Church as a servant. The Church is our servant and not our master. The Church serves us precisely by reminding us always of those promises which surpass every human desire. In the end, anything less than the fulfillment of those promises is a deep and profound disappointment to the human spirit. Think about it. If ever you feel that life is empty and futile, if ever you feel, "Is it really worth going on?" it's perhaps because what we are looking at are those things that cannot fulfill the human desire. That empty feeling means that we are looking at and paying attention to things without God being above all.

As we celebrate this Holy Mass, let us ask the Lord to grant us the grace for which we pray in that beautiful Collect prayer. In fact, this week there have been so many saints that we only rarely got to say the prayer, but it's been there all week. So, let us make that prayer our own in answer to this preaching of Jesus in which he tells us that we are truly free, remembering that freedom comes from listening to the authentic servant voice of the Church—the voice that reminds us always, as Christ himself did, of our hearts.

November 22, 2015
The Solemnity Our Lord Jesus Christ, King of the Universe

READINGS

First Reading: Daniel 7:13-14
Second Reading: Revelation 1:5-8
Gospel Reading: John 18:33B-37

COLLECT

Almighty ever-living God, whose will is to restore all things in your beloved Son, the King of the universe, grant, we pray, that the whole creation, set free from slavery, may render your majesty service and ceaselessly proclaim your praise. Through our Lord Jesus Christ, your Son, who lives and reigns with you in the unity of the Holy Spirit, one God, for ever and ever.

Amen to the Kingship of Christ

Today, the last Sunday in the liturgical year, we celebrate this great feast of Christ the King. This feast is our conclusion. Having contemplated throughout the entire liturgical year first Jesus' journey in his mother's womb, his infancy, his public life, his passion, his death, and his resurrection and then considering and concluding all these things, we recognize, acknowledge, and acclaim Christ as our King.

What exactly does this title *Christ as King* mean? We don't really have kings these days with which we can compare the Kingship of Christ. The first reading from the prophet Jeremiah helps us to understand the sort of king that Jesus is. It says:

> One like the Son of Man coming on the clouds of heaven, one like the Son of Man receiving honor, glory, and kingship. All peoples and nations serve him. His dominion is an everlasting dominion.

This is the kingship of Jesus Christ and it is a fact. If we go to the Gospel, one of the things we see straight away is Jesus answering Pilate that he came into the world to testify to the truth. This is the way Jesus affirms the validity of that title of king that he has received and that has been reported to Pilate.

The first lesson we can learn from this is that the recognition of Jesus as King is not something we give to Jesus. It is not a reward that we give to Jesus, but an acknowledgment of the true place that Jesus has. You can almost hear Jesus saying, "If I were not to proclaim myself king, I would be lying to you. I would not be a witness to the truth."

We've commented before about giving God a place in our lives. I've often said to you, you know you can give your dog a place in your life, you can give your books or your computer a place in your life, but you cannot give God a place in your life. All that you can do with God is acknowledge and recognize that he is supreme, that he is all in all. It's a recognition; it's not an assignment. Jesus as King is not something we give Christ. It is the recognition of who Christ is. It is the recognition of a profound truth about who Christ is. That is why this feast is celebrated on the last Sunday of the year, because it is the conclusion of our human heart and our human reason. After the whole journey of the liturgical year, we conclude by acknowledging this great sovereignty of Jesus our Savior.

Let's look at Pilate, because he is very interesting in this Gospel. The first thing to notice is that he gets it wrong from the very beginning. When interviewing Jesus, Jesus asks him, "Well, what do you say?" Jesus is turning the question back on Pilate. Pilate says, "Am I a Jew?" He is not a Jew. Little did he, the chief representative of the Roman Empire in Palestine at the time, know that it would be just a few short centuries before that entire empire would kneel on front of Jesus and recognize him as Lord and Savior as the Roman world was converted to Christ in those first centuries. So, here, Pilate thinks he can exclude himself from the Jesus question because he is not a member of Israel. But that question is a question for every human being. It's not a question that can be set aside. It's not a question that's for a sector, or a group, or a character type. The issue of the kingship of Christ is a question for everybody.

Then what sort of kingship of Christ is this? Pilate is worried by this title, *king*. The people who are handing Jesus over know that they can use this. They perhaps intuit from the whole tradition that this title of king is not a claim to political power. Yet they are using this because they know this is the trap by which they can snare Pilate and draw him into their plans. Pilate does fall into this trap, and he begins his interrogation of Jesus immediately on this question of kingship. "Are you a problem for Rome? Are you proclaiming a kingdom separate from the authority of Rome?" That's what Pilate wants to know. Is this a political kingdom? Is this a revolution? Is this a new face of anti-Romanism? "My kingdom," Jesus says, "does not belong to this world. If my kingdom did belong to this world my attendants would be fighting to keep me from being handed over. But as it is, my kingdom is not here." Pilate then said to him, "Are you a king?" Jesus is a king and he acknowledges that it is the truth. He must cry out that he is a king. But what sort of kingship is that?

Here we can go to the scene that we have often commented on, of Peter outside the synagogue of Capernaum. Jesus has just spoken about the Eucharist, and so many of his people have left thinking he's crazy and gone away. And Jesus, coming out of the synagogue sees the little group of his apostles there huddled in intense conversation, and he comes over and he says to them, "Are you also going to leave?" (John 6:67) And Peter answers, "No, to whom else would we go?" (John 6:68) I used to think, as a teenager and as a young man, "What a wimpish answer that is." No affirmation of Jesus, no enthusiasm, just "There's nowhere better, so we might as well stay with you." The more I have lived with this phrase and the more I have contemplated and meditated on this phrase, the more I realize that Peter actually says what remains over time to be the most vital and essential thing.

What is Peter's answer? Peter's answer is exactly the recognition of that kingship to which Jesus lays claim. That's why I bring that scene up today, because Peter recognizes, "Lord, in this whole wide world, there is nowhere that we could go where we would find the fullness of life we have found in you. There is nowhere we could go where we could find the happiness, peace, and correspondence of heart that we have found with you. No, Jesus, nothing will separate us from you because you have won our hearts. You have won over our hearts to you."

When he was raised upon the cross, Jesus said that he would draw us all to himself. The cross is the greatest symbol of his kingship. At Mass last night we admitted people into the Catechumenate. Every step of the way was marked by the cross. First, I traced the cross on their foreheads, then their sponsors traced the cross on each of their members as they were blessed. Then each one of them received around their neck the gift of a cross. My friends, the cross is integral to the victory of Christ and to his kingship. He is a crucified king. If we think about the sovereignty of Christ while forgetting the cross, then we misunderstand the victory of Christ. The victory of Christ is the victory he won in the soul of Peter. It is the victory he seeks to win in the soul of each one of us. He wants to draw us to himself, so that through him, we can be reconciled with our heavenly Father. That reconciliation, that call of Christ, is a call that he makes to each one of us. If he were here today, Jesus might say to us, "Do you want to leave me? Do you want to leave the Catholic Church? Do you want to throw off all the shackles of the Catholic Church? Do you want to just go out there and do it your own way and forget all this Catholic stuff? Is that what you want?" My friends, our faith has to grow and deepen to the level in which we can say without hesitation, with Peter, "No, Lord, we do not want anything other than to be with you here. No, Lord, there are many interesting things going on in the world, there are many different movements we could join, and be part of, but we know that none of them gives us an iota of what we have received from you. And, therefore, Lord, no, we will not be separated from you."

My friends, this is the kingship of Christ. The kingship of Christ is this dominion of hearts won to communion with God. And this is the kingship that shall never be destroyed, in the words of the prophet Daniel. This is the kingship that will never tumble or be toppled or overcome by force. The kingdom of those whose hearts are won by Christ. And my friends, our presence here around the altar is exactly that. There really aren't any more Sunday Christians. There aren't any more people who go to Mass because their neighbor is looking. In fact you would be tempted to not go to Mass because your neighbor is looking with the mentality of today.

So, my friends, the affirmation of our presence here on this celebration of Christ the King is exactly the same as Peters' affirmation. We are in the best place. We simply have chosen, this Sunday morning, to come to the very best place that there is. There is no better place. There is no other place. In fact, it is either here or it is nothing. Either here or life becomes a desert; empty, useless, and futile. Life becomes a quiet desperation. Instead, here, life is filled. "Hope does not disappoint," Saint Paul said in the second reading. No, my friends, there is only one hope that does not disappoint. While every other hope disappoints and betrays, this hope endures forever. This hope fulfills and answers. This is why we gather here, and this is why in conclusion of a year of the life of the Church, we proclaim, with great solemnity, and with great joy, the kingdom of Jesus Christ; his kingship. That is why we have the beautiful music of this wonderful choir and orchestra who perform for us. That is why we celebrate with incense and all the solemnity that the liturgy offers. We do it because it's our way.

You could think of the Feast of Christ the King as the "Amen" that you say when you receive the host. In saying that Amen you give the assent of your humanity and your freedom to everything that is communicated as that host is offered to you. When you receive the body of Christ, you say, "Amen." This Feast of Christ the King is our great Amen at the conclusion of the Church's year. Next week when we meet, it will be the first Sunday of Advent and we will begin that journey again in the life of the liturgy. Today, we say with great joy and solemnity, our "Amen." That is the meaning of our celebration today. Let us rejoice and participate with fullness of heart.

November 25, 2016
Friday of the Thirty-fourth Week in Ordinary Time

READINGS

First Reading: Revelation 20:1-4, 11-21:2
Gospel Reading: Luke 21:29-33

COLLECT

Almighty ever-living God, who gave Saint Catherine of Alexandria to your people as a Virgin and an invincible Martyr, grant that through her intercession we may be strengthened in faith and constancy and spend ourselves without reserve for the unity of the Church. Through our Lord Jesus Christ, your Son, who lives and reigns with you in the unity of the Holy Spirit, one God, for ever and ever.

The Grace to Be Another Christ

I remember the day when I was praying and meditating and reading about a saint, and it finally dawned on me that the second coming of the Lord is something to be looked forward to, not something to be dreaded. We can't but long and yearn for the coming of our Lord and for the completion of the great work of history. The Collect prayer said in the last week of the year helps us to understand that we have a part to play in the coming of the Lord. We have a part in preparing for his coming, and that part is the continuation of his work. Jesus came to reconcile the world with his Father. That's the theological part of Jesus' mission; the great work of reconciliation with the Father.

Now, by his passion, death, and resurrection, he provided all the grace and all the blessing necessary for the completion of that task. As I have often said, Jesus didn't violate our freedom. When Jesus died and rose from the dead, he ascended to the right hand of the Father and sent his Holy Spirit to dwell with us. However, he didn't just resolve the issue of history in one fell swoop. Yes, he won the grace for the resolution of the human question, but we still have a role to play because we have to say "Yes." The Lord will not violate our freedom. Therefore, he offers us the abundance of graces that he won through his passion, death, and resurrection. Jesus says, "Come, take, receive, let the work be completed. Let the reconciliation of humanity with God be completed."

First and foremost, our work is to receive that grace ourselves. It is to say "Yes" to Christ ourselves. This is not some fundamental choice that we make one day in our lives, but rather it is a daily struggle. When we get out of bed every morning we have to say "Yes" again. We have to say "Yes" and accept the grace that he has for us that day. At the end of the day we have to gather with him in our heart and tell him we are sorry for the graces that we rejected during the day.

It is by this daily journey, drawing ever closer to him, and being attracted evermore decisively to his grace, that we play the first and most important part in bringing to completion the work of Christ our Savior. He invites us also to join with him in reaching out to others and being missionaries to the world. In other words, he invites us to be other Christs. This is one of the first things I remember hearing as a teenager; that Christians are another Christ. I was kind of shocked. How could we be another Christ? We are another Christ in the sense that, bearing the grace of Baptism and the sanctifying life in our souls, we can touch people. Each one of us is not only able to, but also we could say commissioned to, go out and touch other people with the grace of Christ. Pope Francis continues to urge us on to this apostolic work, to this missionary work, to touch others with the love of Christ and the grace of Christ that is in us. In this way we also help to bring to completion the work that Christ started. Saint Paul tells us that we need to make up what is lacking. It's been commented that if it wasn't Saint Paul who said it, that it would be considered a heresy. But Saint Paul did say it, and therefore it's not a heresy. It is an actual part of the way God wants things done. It is an actual part of the way that God designed to save us– by inviting us to really play a part in the salvation of the world. Through the grace of our baptism, which is the grace that flows from the Paschal mystery, and through the grace renewed in us continually, through the sacraments, especially the sacrament of the Eucharist, we transform this world. We really do transform this world so that the people of today will be no less fortunate than the people of 2,000 years ago who could meet Jesus on the road. Through our presence, the presence of the baptized in the world, Jesus may be encountered still today. Through our presence we may be capable of changing lives, as Jesus changed the life of Zacchaeus.

As we celebrate our Holy Mass, let us ask, that first of all we might receive the grace that Jesus has won for us. Let us ask that we might not be an obstacle to the accomplishment in our own hearts of the salvific work that Jesus carried out by his passion, death, and resurrection. Let us ask that receiving him, and living in and with him, we may be a sign to the world, so that the world can see that our Savior is still alive.

November 28, 2015
Saturday of the Thirty-fourth Week in Ordinary Time

READINGS

First Reading: Daniel 7:15-27
Gospel Reading: Luke 21:34-36

COLLECT

Stir up the will of your faithful, we pray, O Lord, that striving more eagerly to bring your divine work to fruitful completion, they may receive in greater measure the healing remedies your kindness bestows. Through our Lord Jesus Christ, your Son, who lives and reigns with you in the unity of the Holy Spirit, one God, for ever and ever.

The Surface of an Immense Love

This Thanksgiving Day feast is indeed a marvelous feast. It expresses one of the absolutely fundamental positions of the human heart on front of this extraordinary gift of life we have received. We perceive this reality every time we are minimally aware of what is around us. An attitude of thankfulness springs immediately to the heart of one who is truly simple on front of the experience of human existence. Very often we are eager to express our gratitude for the many fortunate things that happen in our life. Indeed, it should be so. However, we must also remember that these good things that happen to us in our life are signs of deeper gifts for which we must be grateful. In the funeral liturgy there is a prayer that says:

> We thank you for the gifts which you bestowed upon the deceased in this life. They are the signs of your goodness.

The goodness of God is something that goes extremely deep. It is worthwhile taking a moment on this Thanksgiving morning to contemplate, just very briefly, the very depths of the goodness of God.

Saint Paul was already right there in his act of thanksgiving that we heard in the second reading. He was thanking God by saying that he will always give thanks to God for the gift of regeneration in those people to whom he preached the Gospel received in Jesus Christ. This is one of the great gifts. Before even that, I think we need to contemplate the very gift of humanity itself. It is truly an extraordinary thing to be a human being. Only in being a human can you begin to say that anything is extraordinary. You know the rocks share this world with us, but they don't marvel at the world in which they exist. We do because we are marvelously made. We are truly stunningly and wonderfully made as creatures of God. We are conceived in a way that goes beyond anything that we can really comprehend.

The Catechism tells us that God made us because he knew we would like being when we existed. Who can even get their mind around that mystery? Yet it's true. God made us for perfect love. He made us not only because he loved us, but so that we could in some way experience, know, be comforted, and live in that love. Indeed, we can even become participants in his love. My friends, this is something extraordinary.

This is why Thanksgiving Day isn't only a feast for those for whom things are going well. Perhaps you yourselves know, as I know, many people who are suffering or dealing with grave hardships on this day. People are suffering right here in our community. Do they cancel Thanksgiving because they are having a hard time or because something tragic happened in the past days in their lives? Do they cancel Thanksgiving because they are facing a major difficulty? If all we notice are the immediate good circumstances, then perhaps we run the risk of thinking that's the way it should be. It is precisely when we contemplate these greater gifts that we can understand an attitude of Thanksgiving and of relationship. Thanksgiving is the acknowledgement of a giver.

The more we realize the immensity of the gift we have received, the more we realize that we can't just stop at the wrapper. Imagine if you gave your kids some gift that you had been saving up for for quite a while because you knew your kids really wanted it. Imagine that you didn't have the money for it so for six months before Christmas you were saving up to be able to give your kid this gift. Then imagine that your kid opens the gift and goes over into the corner with the paper. Your child starts looking at the paper, leaving the gift and ignoring it. You'd say, "Hey, wait a minute, this is the gift. That's just the wrapper. This is the gift."

We have to understand that the many benefits, gifts, and fortunate things that we can mention are just the wrapper. Hopefully we will mention with gratitude on this Thanksgiving Day the gifts that God has bestowed upon us in this year. But they are the wrapper. They are the surface of an immense love with which we were created and which then revealed its face to us in the person of Jesus our Savior. It is extraordinary to think—it's something that we can't even entirely get our minds around—that our God, the creator of all things, the origin of all things, the origin of our very lives, sent his son into the world to share our condition in everything and to draw us into a relationship of love with him. That he embraced the experience of death, for and with us, and that he now lives, giving us life and enriching us.

Remember Saint Paul's beautiful act of thanksgiving that we heard in the second reading. Let us ask that even while we contemplate the many benefits, graces, and gifts received throughout this year, that we might also acknowledge the extraordinary love of God, which he reveals to us always. Let us root ourselves in the extraordinary movement of God's love that has enveloped our lives and that has drawn us entirely to himself. My friends, our God holds nothing, nothing, back from us. I often repeat the words of Pope Benedict, which he said at the beginning of his pontificate. Pope Benedict's words are somewhat less known than John Paul II's great words, "Throw open wide the doors of your hearts to Christ."[22] Although these words are often repeated, Pope Benedict's words are equally a great and beautiful invitation. He says:

> Don't be afraid of God. God comes to take nothing from you, and he withholds nothing from you that can contribute even one iota to your happiness.[23]

Let us ask that as we recognize the very constitutive gifts of blessings and graces from God throughout this year, that we might not stop at the sign, but that we might always continue on the journey to that of which the sign is a sign. The sign points to that for which our hearts are yearning and longing. Let us ask for this grace then, for ourselves and one another as we go on to celebrate this great and marvelous feast so appropriate to our human spirit.

---

22 "*Homily of His Holiness John Paul II for the Inauguration of His Pontificate,*" Saint Peter's Square, Rome, Vatican, October 22, 1978.

23 "*Homily of His Holiness Benedict XVI for the Inauguration of His Pontificate,*" Saint Peter's Square, Rome, Vatican, April 24, 2005.

CPSIA information can be obtained
at www.ICGtesting.com
Printed in the USA
BVHW060515110922
646601BV00005B/19

9 781941 457122